Objectives of Learning Environment

Objectives of Learning Environment

Edited by

Dr.A.MARIYAMMAL

Assistant professor,

Sakthi institute of Teacher Education
and research, Dindigul, Tamil Nadu

RANDOM

RANDOM PUBLICATIONS

NEW DELHI (INDIA)

Objectives of Learning Environment

ISBN 978-93-5111-750-6

Published in 2015 in India by

RANDOM PUBLICATIONS

4376-A/4B, Gali Murari Lal, Ansari Road

New Delhi-110 002

Phone : +9111-43580356, 011-43142548, 011-23289044

e-mail : sales@randompublications.com

info@randompublications.com

randomexports@gmail.com

Type Setting by : Shah Computer Graphics, Delhi-110094

Printed at: Thomson Press (India) Ltd.

Contents

8

9

20

Teaching with Technology and Transforming Learning 179

21

Use of Ict in Teaching- Learning & Evaluation 185

22

Effectiveness of Computer Based Multimedia Learning Material 195

25

Learning without Limit **229**

26

Awareness of Flipped Classroom Among International School Teachers **239**

27

Goal of Learning Environment of Tomorrow **249**

1

Cloud Computing

Introduction

Computer-based multimedia could include several forms of media-audio, text, graphics, and video or film. With computer-based training, the role of both the student and the instructor change. Students become more involved in their own learning, and instructors may no longer occupy a center-stage position in a typical classroom setting. Something similar is happening today in the world of computing. Data and programs are being swept up from desktop PCs and corporate server rooms and installed in "the compute cloud". In general, there is shift in the geography of computation. What is cloud computing exactly? As a beginning here is a definition

"An emerging computer paradigm where data and services reside in massively scalable datacenters in the cloud and can be accessed from any connected devices over the internet" Like other definitions of topics like these, an understanding of the term cloud computing requires an understanding of various other terms which are closely related to this. While there is a lack of precise scientific definitions for many of these terms, general definitions can be given. Cloud computing is an emerging paradigm in the computer industry where the computing is moved to a cloud of computers. It has become one of the buzz words of the industry. The core concept of cloud computing is, quite simply, that the vast computing resources that we need will reside somewhere out there in the cloud of computers and we'll connect to them and use them as and when needed.

Computing can be described as any activity of using and/or developing computer hardware and software. It includes everything that sits in the bottom layer, i.e. everything from raw compute power to storage capabilities. Cloud computing ties together all these entities and delivers them as a single integrated entity under its own sophisticated management. Cloud is a term used as a metaphor for the wide area networks (like internet) or any such large networked environment. It came partly from the cloud-like symbol used to represent the complexities of the networks in the schematic diagrams.

Cloud Computing

Cloud Computing is the internet-based storage for files, applications, and infrastructure. One could say cloud computing has been around for many years, but now a company may buy or rent space for their daily operations.

The cost savings in implementing a cloud system is substantial and the pricing for use of cloud computing can easily be scaled up or down as determined by necessity.

A definition for cloud computing can be given as an emerging computer paradigm where data and services reside in massively scalable data centers in the cloud and can be accessed from any connected devices over the internet. Cloud computing is a way of providing various services on virtual machines allocated on top of a large physical machine pool which resides in the cloud. Cloud computing comes into focus only when we think about what IT has always wanted – a way to increase capacity or add different capabilities to the current setting on the fly without investing in new infrastructure, training new personnel or licensing new software. Here 'on the fly' and 'without investing or training' becomes the keywords in the current situation. But cloud computing offers a better solution. We have lots of compute power and storage capabilities residing in the distributed environment of the cloud. What cloud computing does is to harness the capabilities of these resources and make available these resources as a single entity which can be changed to meet the current needs of the user. The basis of cloud computing is to create a set of virtual servers on the available vast resource pool and give it to the clients. Any web enabled device can be used to access the resources through the virtual servers. Based on the computing needs of the client, the infrastructure allotted to the client can be scaled up or down. From a business point of view, cloud computing is a method to address the scalability and availability concerns for large scale applications which involves lesser overhead. Since the resource allocated to the client can be varied based on the needs of the client and can be done without any fuss, the overhead is very low. One of the key concepts of cloud computing is that processing of 1000 times the data need not be 1000 times harder. As and when the amount of data increases, the cloud computing services can be used to manage the load effectively and make the processing tasks easier. In the era of enterprise servers and personal computers, hardware was the commodity as the main criteria for the processing capabilities depended on the hardware configuration of the server. But with the advent of cloud computing, the commodity has changed to cycles and bytes - i.e. in cloud computing services, the users are charged based on the number of cycles of execution performed or the number of bytes transferred.

Characteristics of Cloud Computing

Multi-tenancy

With cloud computing, any application supports multi-tenancy - that is multiple tenants at the same instant of time. The system allows several customers to share the infrastructure allotted to them without any of them being aware of the sharing. This is done by virtualizing the servers on the available machine pool and then allotting the servers to multiple users.

Service-oriented

Cloud computing systems are all service oriented - i.e. the systems are such that they are created out of other discrete services. Many such Cloud Computing discrete services which are independent of each other are combined together to form this service. This allows re-use of the different services that are available and that are being created.

Virtualized

The applications in cloud computing are fully decoupled from the underlying hardware. The cloud computing environment is a fully virtualized environment.

Flexible

Another feature of the cloud computing services is that they are flexible. They can be used to serve a large variety of workload types - varying from small loads of a small consumer application to very heavy loads of a commercial application.

Need for Cloud Computing

What could we do with 1000 times more data and CPU power? One simple question. That's all it took the interviewers to bewilder the confident job applicants at Google. This is a question of relevance because the amount of data that an application handles is increasing day by day and so is the CPU power that one can harness. There are many answers to this question. With this much CPU power, we could scale our businesses to 1000 times more users. Right now we are gathering statistics about every user using an application. With such CPU power at hand, we could monitor every single user click and every user interaction such that we can gather all the statistics about the user. We could improve the recommendation systems of users. We could model better price plan choices. With this CPU power we could simulate the case where we have say 1, 00,000 users in the system without any glitches. There are lots of other things we could do with so much CPU power and data capabilities. But what is keeping us back.

Uses of Cloud Computing

1. Rapid Service
2. Secure Service

3. Satisfying User Experience
4. Lower Costs
5. Multi-User Access
6. Development Platform
7. Infinite Storage

Speed

Use cloud computing to innovate fast. Quickly build cloud applications. Tap into pay-for-use global cloud infrastructure.

Economics

Save time with self-service cloud. Buy just what you need. Get to market faster. Shift CAPEX to OPEX. Increase utilisation.

Cloud Computing in the Real World

Time Machine

Times machine is a New York Times project in which one can read any issue from Volume 1, Number 1 of The New York Daily Times, on September 18, 1851 through to The New York Times of December 30, 1922. They made it such that one can choose a date in history and flip electronically through the pages, displayed with their original look and feel. Here's what they did. They scanned all their public domain articles from 1851 to 1992 into TIFF files.

Conclusion

Cloud computing is a powerful new abstraction for large scale data processing systems which is scalable, reliable and available. In cloud computing, there are large self-managed server pools available which reduces the overhead and eliminates management headache. Cloud computing services can also grow and shrink according to need. Cloud computing is particularly valuable to small and medium businesses, where effective and affordable IT tools are critical to helping them become more productive without spending lots of money on in-house resources and technical equipment. Also it is a new emerging architecture needed to expand the Internet to become the computing platform of the future.

Reference

1. Google http//: www. Community resources.edu
2. http://www.infoworld.com/article/08/04/07/15FE-cloud-computing-reality_1.html, "What Cloud Computing Really Means"
3. Instructional technology for teaching and learning: Designing instruction, integrating computers, and using media. (2nd ed.) Upper Saddle River, NJ, Merrill
4. Talabi, J. K. (2001). Educational Technology.Accra Universal Press.
5. The World Book Encyclopedia (2001).U.S.A: Onyx.

2

The Use of A Blended Learning Approach Undertaken with A Group of B.ed Trainees

Introduction

Blended learning can be thought of as a pedagogical approach that combines the effectiveness and socialization opportunities of classroom 'with, the technologically advanced, active learning possibilities of the online environment. Research has shown that high level of student and instructor satisfaction can be produced the fully online environment. But both faculty and students lament the loss of face-to-face interaction. But blended learning proves to be an effective step whereby allows a faculty to begin with a course that is mostly face-to-face, and then switch it over to the online component as soon as the students' expertise in the field increases. Blended-learning, the combination of traditional face-to-face teaching methods with authentic online learning activities has the potential to transform student learning experiences and outcome.

What is Blended Learning?

Blended Learning is a combination of face-to-face instruction and online instruction. Using the provincial Learning Management

System (LMS), students and teachers in regular classrooms can access high-quality course content and use secure online tools such as the Calendar, Drop box, News, Discussion, Blogs, Journal and Surveys. Blended Learning combines the support of a classroom teacher while allowing students the opportunity to develop skills essential for success in the 21st century.

A few of the many definitions of blended learning include

1. The integration of face-to-face and online learning to help enhance the classroom experience and extend learning through the innovative use of information and communications technology. Blended strategies enhance student engagement and learning through online activities to the course curriculum, and improve effectiveness and efficiencies by reducing lecture time.
2. A course that blends online and face-to-face delivery. Substantial proportion of the content is delivered online, typically uses online discussions, and typically has some face-to-face meetings. The Sloan Consortium defines blended courses as having between 30 percent and 79 percent of their content delivered online, with the remaining portion of the course content delivered by face-to-face instruction or other non web-based methods, such as paper textbooks.

In other words, blended learning should be approached not merely as a temporal construct, but rather as a fundamental redesign of the instructional model with the following characteristics:

1. A shift from lecture to student centered instruction in which students become active and interactive learners.
2. Increases in interaction between student-instructor, student-student, student-content, and student-outside resources;
3. Integrated formative and summative assessment mechanisms for students and instructor.

Most universities today recognize that there are particular learning needs for the students. Students entering university courses often need to develop a number of skills and capabilities to achieve success. The students come from a range of previous positions including school, the workplace and often unemployment. Students quickly need to be able to assume responsibility for their own learning, to undertake independent research and inquiry, and to communicate and argue their ideas in a succinct fashion.

Blended-Learning Approach

Blended-learning describes an approach to learning where teachers use technology, usually in the form of Web-based instruction, in concert with and as a supplement to live instruction, or perhaps utilize components of a learner-centered Web course with components that require significant instructor presence and guidance. The strength of a blended-learning approach is that it provides a means to ensure learners are supported and guided as they undertake independent learning tasks.

e - TQM College Blended Learning Approach

Use of the Web in such settings provides many affordances for the teacher and students in the form of communication channels, information sources and management tools. These aspects appear to make blended-learning particularly well suited to teacher training students, especially those in large groups where direct instructor support may be difficult to deliver Blended-learning commonly describes learning that combines traditional teaching and learning approaches with information and communication technologies. It is anticipated that blended-learning will enhance the student learning experience. A typical example of this would be blending online activities with face—to-face sessions. This can mean using the best of the best - the best use of online learning to enable classroom activities to be active and engaging learning experiences (Graham, 2006)

Blended learning consists of two features

1. It is a planned combination of online learning and Face- to-Face (F2F) instruction using a variety of learning resources.
2. It is an educational format that integrates online learning techniques including online delivery of materials through web pages, discussion boards, and e-mail with traditional teaching.

Ingredients of Blended Learning

1. **Live Events:** Synchronous, teacher-led learning environment in which all learners participate at the same time. It can be in real classroom or can be virtual.
2. **Self-paced learning:** Recorded live events, Internet based or CD ROM based, which helps the learner to learn at his own pace.
3. **Collaboration:** It implies a more dynamic communication and interaction among many learners that brings about knowledge sharing.
4. **Assessment:** It is both live and online measure of learner's knowledge to determine prior knowledge as well as to measure learning transfer
5. **Performance Support:** These are reference materials that enhance learning, retention and transfer. It may be printable references, downloaded multimedia learning objects, documentations etc.

More effective pedagogy

While there is no formula that will guarantee learning for every student in every context, there is extensive, well-documented evidence about the kinds of teaching approaches that consistently have a positive impact on student learning. This evidence tells us that students learn best when teachers: create a supportive learning environment Thus blended-learning provide opportunities for:

1. more increase in active learning strategies
2. more learner-centered focus
3. a greater emphasis on peer to-peer learning.
4. a change in the way faculty allocate time for increased mentoring of individual students
5. Innovative instruction.
6. the possibility for interaction with remote expert or peer review of projects

7. enhance the relevance of new learning
8. facilitate shared learning of mathematics
9. make connections to prior learning and experience
10. Allows for more creative and interactive course assignments.

Access to knowledge

6. Assist the making of connections by enabling students to enter and explore new learning environments, overcoming barriers of distance and time.
7. Facilitate shared learning by enabling students to join or create communities of learners that extend well beyond the classroom.
8. Assist in the creation of supportive learning environments by offering resources that take account of individual, cultural, or developmental differences.
9. Enhance opportunities to learn by offering students virtual experiences and tools that save them time, allowing them to take their learning further.

Smart Classrooms

Smart Classrooms are technology enhanced classrooms that foster opportunities for teaching and learning by integrating learning technology, such as computers, specialized software, audience response technology, networking, and audio/visual capabilities. The smart classrooms demand learning initiative that assists educators to make ICT integral to learning. The strategy is about engaging the digital generation, improving individualized learning opportunities, sparking innovation in learning, enhancing teachers' digital pedagogy and getting the best from schools' ICT investment. The challenge lies in shifting from teaching and learning about ICT to teaching and learning with and through ICT. This means rather than using technology to do old things in new Ways, we want to do new things in new ways and use technology to enable and transform teaching, learning and the curriculum.

Smart Classrooms vis-a-vis Blended Learning

Smart classroom uses following elements, mixed in varied proportions according to an organization's requirements of blended learning:

Learning through information

Material based information is the first coherent step towards starting a learning program. Web based material can now be handed to the learners, thanks to e-learning techniques, which can render the learning program easy to deliver and faster to implement. Making the information accessible all the time will give learners the liberty of scrolling through the content at their own convenience, which, in turn, will enhance understanding and enthusiasm.

Learning through interaction

The learner- instructor, learner-content, learner-learner, and Learner-infrastructure interactions become all the more important in a blended-learning environment. Web can assist all the above mentioned forms of interaction, which, together, help retain the knowledge that is acquired through information .Web simulations of real life situations allow learners to apply their knowledge practically, without the possibility of them affecting your business directly.

Learning through collaboration

Collaborative learning includes peer-to-peer discussions, conference calls, chat, team rooms and instant messaging. Technology has enhanced the concept of collaboration manifold, where learners, even though geographically remote, can communicate in real time. The collaborative environment also heightens the chances of collaboration between e-learners and subject matter experts (SMEs).

Learning through classroom interactions

Conventional, tested and, by far, one of the most effective approaches to learning, classrooms are the best places to personally connect to peers and instructors. N o technology can replace the advantages of this approach, which is exactly why no e-learning or blended-learning model will skip this element for any reason. But, as one would like to believe, blended learning has never attempted to replace classroom based learning. On the contrary, technology-based learning takes care of the basic, mechanical and mundane aspects of learning to allow classroom-based training centre around discussions on already learnt subject matter and behavioral and psychological modifications.

e-learning technology can be put to good use while learning through information, interaction and collaboration. This not only reduces cost attributed to enlarged periods of non-productive activity on the part of the employees, commuting and employing instructors, but also creates reusable content, and reiterates core messages and concepts to ingrain them in the minds of the learners. At the same time, the classroom sessions develop interpersonal skills and the ability to communicate face-to-face.

Potential constituents of a blended learning approach: The notion of blending is nothing new. Good classroom teachers have always blended their methods -reading, writing, lecture, discussion, practice and projects, to name just a few, are all part of an effective blend. As has already been discussed, blended-learning arrangements tend to combine an electronic learning component with some form of human intervention; the constituents may vary in different settings. As is clear, the medium is not limited to technology and can include: Stand-alone, Asynchronous, or Synchronous online learning/training ; Performance support tools (knowledge management tools); Traditional classroom, labs, or other 'hands-on' experiences; Reading assignments, CD-ROM or other self- paced learning; Tele-training,Tele-learning, or Other media. Here is a table that categorizes the type of learning that may be used:

Video/DVD

Blended learning can include technology as common place today as using a video/DVD clip, segment, or movie. Videos used in classroom settings, regardless who produced them, can be educational, promotional, training, event, and evaluative.

Virtual Fieldtrips

Blended learning Virtual Fieldtrips can be used in any number of ways to serve a variety of educational goals. Using blended learning through the virtual field trip is a wonderful opportunity. The virtual field trip experience is an excellent model of a teaching strategy that was not possible before the advent of computers in the classroom.

Interactive Websites

Blended learning often includes the use of interactive websites. The use of interactive websites requires computer and Internet access in the learning situation. These sites provide another opportunity for teachers to use technology in their classroom, thus promoting blended learning. Interactive websites can be utilized within the class for those students who do not have Internet access and can give other students the opportunity to expand knowledge if access is available privately.

Websites for Teachers

Classroom websites help facilitate the creation of a blended-learning environment. Teachers use classroom websites to post assignments, receive homework submissions, administer tests, and post grades and classroom policies. Teachers also use classroom websites as the medium to link to blended- learning sites such as external websites, videos, software, graphics, audio feeds, and virtual field trips.

Course Management Systems

The use of a Course Management System (CMS) can assist a teacher when he or she is creating a blended learning environment in the classroom. In addition to using a classroom website to communicate and administer classroom activities (as described in the previous section), a CMS can better assess student work, share course content and help develop a community among the teachers, students, and parents. A CMS allows for the administration of blended activities into the classroom through various tools included with the software.

The success of a blend largely depends on the right mix of the elements. A good blend would provide optimum role of live interaction. It is essential to provide a good support and training model and should keep the cultural components in mind. A successful blend would strike the right balance between innovations and mass utility. Some of the basic factors which should be considered in identifying the blend are:

1. Course instructional goals
2. Student profile
3. Hours of learning/training
4. Teacher experience and teaching style
5. Cultural dimensions
6. Resource availability
7. Budgetary requirement for training implementation

What Kind of Learners we Require?

1. Demonstrate creativity and intellectual curiosity resulting in enjoyment, fun and resilience.
2. Exhibit a sense of self-confidence and enjoyment.
3. Are self directed and can work independently, collaboratively and cooperatively to learn and to develop products of use with themselves and others.
4. Display innovation and entrepreneurship.
5. Continually develop communication and collaboration skills.
6. Communicate globally through e-learning spaces.
7. Are able to research effectively and have information ûuency.
8. Have developed digital literacy and understand technology operations and concepts.
9. Have developed digital proficiency to work effectively in 21st Century environments.
10. Understand digital citizenship and work on issues and challenges that are real and relevant, that make a difference to them and to others.

11. Demonstrate accountability and adaptability.
12. Have developed skills to design, create, share and publish.
13. Build critical and systems thinking enabling problem identification, formulation and solution, and decision making.
14. Use ICT purposefully to engage in real research.
15. Explore new ideas and tools in authentic contexts.

What Kind of Teachers we Require?

1. Demonstrate an ongoing commitment to professional knowledge, professional practice, professional relationships and professional values.
2. Have understanding of the transformative role of ICT for 21st Century curriculum design/interpretation, pedagogy and student learning.
3. Make conscious decisions about student learning based on an understanding of digital learners.
4. Are lifelong learners who are willing to take risks, fail and explore areas outside his or her expertise?
5. Employ a variety of methodologies, current learning theories and practices.
6. Constantly collaborate with colleagues and practicing professionals in order to consolidate understanding and to share and reflect on their learning, wonderings and discoveries.

Challenges

The challenges in a blended-learning environment can be looked in two different perspectives –learner perspective and teacher perspective. In focusing on the learner perspective, there is a need to consider the learning style and perceptual skills and abilities of students while designing blended-learning strategy. Learner's proûciency in using ICT is also important in a blended-learning environment. Therefore determining the skills and the ways students acquire and construct knowledge online is very important while designing blended-learning strategy. From the perspective of pedagogy, teaching and learning in a blended-learning environment can be highly unstable and fluctuating. One of the major challenges the teacher faces while designing a blended-learning strategy is to determine the balance between online and face-to-face instruction. There is a need of great expertise on the part of the teacher to design the strategy by considering both the educational provisions of the institute and the learner's needs in a blended-learning environment. But the issue arises in deciding the balance between online and face-to-face components. There is no unique model and the difficulty resides in identification of the balance point. Therefore it demands high attention on the part of a teacher to design learning environment with appropriate ingredients in correct proportions. It is the responsibility of authorities to provide necessary learning support in providing access to online learning so that our students become 'blended learners' with self-regulatory authentic learning experience.

Conclusion

It is inevitable that campus-based college of educational institutions will adopt blended learning approaches in a significant way. As has been demonstrated by several institutions, once there is clear policy and strong leadership, the evolution will be quick. In a matter of a few short years, college of educational institutions can be transformed in a manner consistent with their values and mitigating the fiscal and pedagogical challenges and deficiencies currently challenging the quality of the classroom experience. The academic benefit, evidence, and competitive advantages are clear; only the will and commitment remains. Blended learning can begin the necessary process of redefining college of educational institutions as being learning centered and facilitating a higher learning experience.

References

1. Allison Rossett, Felicia Dnuglis, and Rebecca V. Frazee. Strategies for Building Blended Learning, http://wwwleamingcircuits.org/2003/jul2003/rossett.htm.

2. Dutta, Subrat. (2003) "Impact of Information Communication Technology on Society." Yojna. 47, no. 7: 24. Ibid. (2003) Yojna. 47, no. 7: 30.
3. Garrison, D.R. & Vaughan, N.D. (2008) Blended learning in higher education: Framework, principles and guidelines, John Wiley and Sons: USA.
4. Lever-Duffy, Judy, McDonald, Jean B.and Mizell, Al P. (2003). Teaching and learning with technology: Allyn and Bacon.
5. NCERT (2005) National curriculum framework 2005, New Delhi: NCERT.
6. Sonkambl, C. & Pagare, P. (2010). Use of blended learning approach in teacher education. In Z. Abasetal. (Eds.), Proceedings of Global Learn Asia Paciûc 2010 (pp. 3978-3981). AAC-E.
7. Takwale, Ram: "Challenges and opportunities of globalization for higher education in India" Alternative through e-education.
8. UNESCO (2005).ICT in schools-A handbook foteachers. Bangkok: UNESCO. 10
9. Cameron, B. (2003). The effectiveness of simulation in a hybrid and online networking course. TechTrends, 4 7(5), 18-21
10. Cottrell, D.M. & Robinson, R.A. (2003). Blended-learning in an accounting course. The Quarterly Review of Distance Education, 4(3), 261-269.

3

Blended Learning

Introduction

Blended Learning is an approach to learning and teaching which combines and aligns learning undertaken in face-to-face sessions with learning opportunities created online. New types of learning activities challenge our thinking as to how learning might be facilitated, creating new etiquettes of learning and teaching, and shifting the locus of control from the teacher to the learner (Littlejohn and Pegler, 2006, p4).

History of blended learning

Technology-based training emerged as an alternative to instructor-led training in the 1960s on mainframes and mini-computers. The major advantage that blended learning offers is scale, whereas one instructor can only teach so many people. One example is PLATO (Programmed Logic for Automatic Teaching Operations), a system developed by the University of Illinois and Control Data. PLATO in particular had a long history of innovations and offered coursework from elementary to the college level. Mainframe-based training had a number of interface limitations that gave way to satellite-based live video in the 1970s. The advantage here was serving people who were not as PC-literate, the major challenge was the expense required to make this work. In the early 1980s, CD-ROMs emerged as a dominant form of providing technology-based learning as bandwidth through 56k modems weren't able to support very high quality sound and video. The limitation to CD-ROMs was tracking completion of coursework, so learning management systems emerged as a way to facilitate progress tracking. The aviation industry used this heavily to track how well one did on courses, how much time was spent, and where someone left off. AICC, Aviation Industry Computer-Based Training Committee, was formed in 1988 and companies such as Boeing used CD-ROMs to provide training for personnel. Modern blended learning is delivered online, although CD-ROMs could feasibly still be used if a learning management system meets an institution's standards. Some examples of channels through which online blending learning can be delivered include webcasting (synchronous and asynchronous) and online video (live and recorded).

The concept of blended learning has been around for a long time, but its terminology was not firmly established until around the beginning of the 21st century, in which multiple learning environments and activities are combined, has existed for quite some time. When the first Handbook of Blended Learning by Bonk and Graham was published. In this publication Graham challenged the breadth and ambiguity of the term's definition, and defined 'blended learning systems' as learning systems that "combine face-to-face instruction with computer mediated instruction." Currently, use of the term blended learning mostly involves "combining Internet and digital media with established classroom forms that require the physical co-presence of teacher and students." Long before the advent of computers and social networks, teachers created blended learning experiences using simple technologies like paper and pencil. Educators have always crafted learning experiences that incorporate a variety of activities in different environments for the purpose of reinforcing learning material. For example, consider the concept of the apprenticeship. Prior to the hands-on experience, the apprentice studied the work of the master through observation, conversation, and possibly through reading.

Contemporary definitions of blended learning take into account the role that technology can play. Technologies like CD-ROM and later the internet made it possible to create new environments for learning, new opportunities for synchronous and asynchronous collaboration, and new modes of delivery for learning materials, self-directed guides, and tutorials. More recently, blended learning figures prominently in conversations about online learning. In this context, blended learning represents a convergence of online and face-to-face experiences. Interactions across both environments are mitigated by space, time, fidelity, and personal interaction.

Word usage and context

The terms "blended," "hybrid," "technology-mediated instruction," "web-enhanced instruction," and "mixed-mode instruction" are often used interchangeably in current research literature. However, recent researchers in the United States tend to use the term "blended learning" with more regularity.

What is blended learning?

A blended learning approach to instruction combines face-to-face classroom methods with computer-based/mediated activities, resulting in an integrated learning experience for students. Blended courses combine face-to-face and online methods to varying degrees, depending on the discipline, the size of the class, student demographics, and the preferences of the instructor. There are no rules in place to prescribe what the ideal blend is.

For example, a blended approach to a traditional, face-to-face course might mean that the class meets once per week instead of the usual three-session format. Learning activities that otherwise would have taken place during classroom time such as lectures, an in-class debate, and a quiz on audio and visual material can be moved online with the help of different tools.

Note that the terms "blended" and "hybrid," tend to be used interchangeably but in current research literature, blended appears more frequently.

Why try a blended approach?

The goal of a blended approach is to leverage the best aspects of both face-to-face and online instruction for the students' benefit. The advantage of using a blended approach is that instead of using classroom time for presentation of material, for example, you can use that time to engage students by handling and clarifying their questions, to help them apply what they view/listen to in lecture, and to work with each other in face-to-face or team problem-solving. As well, online activities and assessments can usually be completed at any time of day, anywhere the student has internet access.

The Definition of Blended Learning

1. "The thoughtful integration of classroom face-to- face learning experiences with online learning experiences"
2. "Blended learning combines online with face-to-face learning. The goal of blended learning is to provide the most efficient and effective instruction experience by combining delivery modalities".
3. "Blended learning - mixed mode or hybrid - learning is the integration of face-to-face (F2F) learning with online learning activities"
4. "A solution that combines several different delivery methods, such as collaboration software, Web-based courses and knowledge management practices"
5. "Learning that mixes various event-based activities, including face-to-face classrooms, live e-learning, and self-paced instruction."
6. "Blended learning is the effective combination of different modes of delivery, models of teaching and styles of learning"
7. Blended learning is the combination of multiple approaches to pedagogy or teaching. For example:- self-paced, collaborative or inquiry-based study
8. A mix of different didactic methods and delivery formats.

Blended learning refers to any time a student learns, at least in part, at a brick and mortar facility through online delivery with student control over time, place, or pace. Blended learning is replacing "e-learning" as the next big thing. Blended learning programs are perhaps the highest impact, lowest cost way to drive major corporate initiatives." Alternative names,

(a) mixed learning

(b) hybrid learning

(c) blended e-learning

(d) melted learning

9. Blended Learning is not so much an innovation as it is a natural by-product of the digital domain creeping into physical boundaries. As digital and social media become more and more prevalent in the life of learners, it was only a matter of time before learning became "blended" by necessity.

10. That said, there's a bit more to Blended and "Hybrid" Learning than throwing in a little digital learning.

Creating a blended learning experience

In a blended learning approach, attention is given to the overall instructional design of the learning experience. While thoughtful planning is essential, blended learning is a fluid process whereby learning needs, moments of insight, and unique pathways evolve. Ideally, the learner is offered more choice in how the learning experience unfolds. This kind of flexibility makes it easier to differentiate instruction, satisfying the needs of a diverse population of learners. Technology is used as a tool for learning and to promote a discovery-based approach to online learning and is not necessary in all blended learning scenarios.

Blended learning is a student-centered approach to creating a learning experience whereby the learner interacts with other students, with the instructor, and with content through thoughtful integration of online and face-to-face environments. A well-designed blended learning experience thoughtfully organizes content, support materials, and activities via synchronous and asynchronous learning events, all of which are delivered in a variety of modes ranging from traditional lecture to online tutorials. Communication and collaboration are necessary functions of a blended approach. Because formative assessment is embedded throughout learning events, the learner assumes responsibility for his or her learning.

In contrast to teacher-cantered, rote-learning approaches, blended learning environments provide multiple ways to access content and to demonstrate mastery. As a result, they lend themselves more readily to differentiation of content and process. A blended approach also gives the learner the opportunity to be more responsible for his or her learning, which creates a learning situation that may be more meaningful on an individual level. Because the learner comes to construct knowledge through personal effort, she or he is more likely to demonstrate understanding beyond rote memorization, and to transfer what she or he has learned to new settings.

(a) To personalize learning, and enhance the motivation for each student.

(b) To increase the reading level.

(c) To help each student master the content and skills they need.

Types of Blended Learning

(a) Face-to-face Driver

(b) Rotation

(c) Flex

(d) Online Lab

(e) Self-Blend

(f) Online Driver

Opportunities

(a) Common Core implementation that leads to deeper learning

(b) Online assessment starting in most states in 2014-15

(c) Competency based systems that make it easier to manage individual progress

(d) Learning environments and adaptive systems that get better as students learn

(e) De-risking the shift to blended learning

(f) Big data: real time dynamic information for teachers and students

(g) Scaled proof points to drive policy change

(h) Public engagement and elevating the debate

Blended Learning Tools

Blended learning uses the tools of the provincial Learning Management System (LMS) to teach and support learning in a face-to-face class. Through blended learning, K-12 students can access high-quality course materials, course calendars, and assignments during and outside school hours.

Students can also take part in face-to-face lessons and communicate with their teacher and classmates using a suite of secure online tools inside the password-protected LMS. These tools help students learn or review key concepts, stay organized, show what they have learned, submit assignments, track their achievement, and communicate with others. This suite of online secure tools includes:

Blog	Calendar	Checklist	Content
Discussions	Dropbox	Email	ePortfolio
Grades	Journal	Locker	News
Pager	Progress	Quizzes	Survey

Blended learning can look different in different situations. For example, when blended learning occurs in a school computer lab, students may flexibly access and complete course content online and consult with their teachers on specific projects or topics. When blended learning occurs in classrooms where technology is limited, students may learn mostly through face-to-face lessons, but use computers or other devices to complete group assignments or submit completed work to their teachers.

Comparing Blended Learning to Other Forms of Learning

Unlike e-learning classes where students are physically separate from their teacher and classmates, blended learning occurs within a face-to-face class that happens at a specific place and time. Blended learning combines the support of classroom learning with the flexibility of e-learning. The following chart shows some examples to clarify how different types of learning and teaching might occur.

Advantages

Proponents of blended learning argue that by incorporating the "asynchronous Internet communication technology" into courses serves to "facilitate a simultaneous independent and collaborative learning experience", and this incorporation is a major contributor to student satisfaction and success in such courses. The use of information and communication technologies has been found to improve access to as well as student attitudes towards learning. By incorporating information technology into class projects, communication between lecturers and part-time students was improved, and students were able to better evaluate their understanding of course material via the use of "computer-based qualitative and quantitative assessment modules" in a study by Alexander and McKenzie (1998).

Disadvantages

Blended learning has a strong dependence on the technical resources with which the blended learning experience is delivered—these tools need to be reliable, easy to use, and up to date in order for the use of the Internet to have a meaningful impact on the learning experience. Additionally, IT literacy can serve as a significant barrier for students attempting to get access to the course materials, making the availability of high quality technical support paramount. It has been observed that the use of lecture recording technologies can result in students falling behind on the material-in a study performed across four different universities, it was found that only half of the students watched the lecture videos on a regular basis, and nearly 40% of students watched several weeks worth of videos in one sitting.

References

1. Garrison, R. & Kanuka, H. (2004). Blended learning: Uncovering its transformative potential in higher education. Internet and Higher Education. 7(2004). P. 95-105.

2. Levonen, J., Joutsenvirta, T. & Parikka, R. 2006. Blended Learning – katsaus sulautuvaan yliopisto-opetukseen. Piirtoheitin 1/06. www.valt.helsinki.fi/piirtoheitin/sulautus1.htm

3. R. Garrison & H. Kanuka, "Blended Learning: Uncovering its Transformative Potential in Higher Education," *Internet and Higher Education* 7 (2004): 95–105.

4. E. Massie, "Blended Learning: The Magic is in the Mix," in *The ASTD E-Learning Handbook*, edited by A. Rossett (New York: McGraw-Hill, 2002), 59.

5. C. Graham, "Blended Learning Systems: Definitions, Current Trends, and Future Directions," in *The Handbook of Blended Learning: Global Perspectives, Local Designs*, edited by C. Bonk & C. Graham (San Francisco, CA: John Wiley & Sons, Inc. 2006).

6. I. Allen, J. Seaman, & R. Garrett, *Blended Learning: The Extent and Promise of Blended Learning in the United States* (Needham, MA: The Sloan Consortium, 2007.)

4

Effectiveness of Blended Learning Programme in Teaching Biology at Higer Secondary School Students

Introduction

The technology is an integral part in the lives of young people who are direct beneficiaries of the educational process. This was often made argument for the need to develop learning methods that use modern technology in the formative and educational. By such methods students are responsible for their own learning, on which they themselves have control and manage it according to their interests and needs. The specialists' researches reveal that the methods which combine the traditional education with the modern technologies (*blended learning*) have increased the effectiveness. Blended Learning is a strategy which integrates the teaching learning process with different learning environments like face-to-face, online, social networking etc. Its rapid growth has been facilitated by the Internet and other emerging technologies like cloud computing, social networking etc. This paper provides a view about the effectiveness of blended learning programme in teaching biology at higher secondary school students

The recent research in science education has focused on instruction that is specific science content, specific instructional strategies and how they are related to biology learning contexts and instructional outcomes. In the present scientific and technological age, the conventional teaching methods are not sufficient to arouse interest among the students and do not meet up to the intellectual, psychological and emotional needs of the students in the new millennium. The methods of teaching biology need to be changed.

In a vast country like India, enormous work is now being done in the field of education but it is still not possible to equip each and every higher and higher secondary school with all the facilities for teaching biology in the near future. Most of the higher secondary schools, both in rural and urban area are suffering from lack of modern science laboratories. They need equally advanced gadgets to support their education. Technology enables students get a live vision of life's aspects and scientific factors. Any diagram can be explained in detail with 3d effect, it helps the student to understand the lesson clearly. Keeping in mind the investigator felt it appropriate to use blended learning for the teaching of the concepts in biology topics included in the XI standard biology syllabus (Tamil Medium).

Blended Learning

Blended learning provides platform to attract the senses of the learner for easy and happy learning. Blended learning is a programme which integrates teaching learning process with different leaning environment. Its rapid growth facilitated by the internet and other emerging technology cloud computing and social networking. "Blended learning is the thoughtful fusion of face-to-face and online learning experiences. The basic principle is that face-to-face oral communication and online written communication are optimally integrated such that the strengths of each are blended into a unique learning experience congruent with the context and intended educational purpose."

Blended learning - an instructional practice that combines teaching methods from both face-to-face instruction and online learning, gives to educational institutions new approaches and strategies for addressing the challenges they face and for taking advantage of the exciting new learning opportunities that are now available.

Blended learning does not exclude the traditional learning methods, but adds new and modern methods as: IT tools (email, web, chat, online conferences, e-learning platforms), workshops, individual project groups, practical demonstrations, etc.

Objectives of the Study

The objectives of the study as follows

1. To find out the effectiveness of blended learning programme for the teaching of biology at higher secondary level.
2. To compare the effectiveness of blended learning programme in the teaching of biology with conventional method of teaching biology.

Hypotheses of the Study

The following null hypotheses have been formulated.

1. There is no significant difference between the experimental group and control group in the achievement of biology at pre test level.
2. There is no significant difference between the experimental group and control group in the achievement of biology at posttest level.
3. There is no significant difference between the pretest and posttest in the achievement of biology for the experimental group.
4. There is no significant difference between the pretest and posttest in the achievement of biology for the control group.

Sample

The sample of the study consists of 100 students studying in XI standard under State Board syllabus at perambalur district. The sample includes both boys and girls.

Tools Used

The following tools had been used for the present study:

An achievement test in biology constructed and validated by the investigators.Blended learning programme was developed by the investigator for the teaching of the concepts in biology topics included in the XI standard biology syllabus.

The progrmme was arranged logically based on the psychological principles of learning. Experimental design was adopted. For the experimentation pretest was conducted and sample was divided into two groups. The students of the experimental group were taught with the blended learning progrmme and the control group through the conventional method. After the treatment period the posttest was administered. The collected data were subjected to statistical analysis and the results obtained were interpreted.

Testing of Hypotheses

Hypothesis 1: There is no significant difference between the experimental group and control group in the achievement of biology at pre test level.

The't' test applied to test the significance of difference between the mean achievement test scores of the experimental group and control group of pretest level.

Table -1

Mean Achievement Test Scores of the Experimental Group Compared with that of the Control Group at Pretest level

Groups	N	Mean	S.D	't' value	Level of Significance at 0.05 level
Experimental	30	20.43	2.09	0.46	Not significant
Control	30	19.63	1.87		

The table indicates that the 't' value is not significant at 0.05 level. The students of the experimental group do not differ significantly from the students of the control group in the mean achievement test scores at pre test level.

Hypothesis 2: There is no significant difference between the experimental group and control group in the achievement of biology at posttest level

Th 't' test applied to test the significance of difference between the mean achievement test scores of the experimental group and control group of posttest level.

Table - 2

Mean Achievement Test Scores of the Experimental Group Compared with that of the Control Group at Posttest level

Groups	N	Mean	S.D	't' value	Level of Significance at 0.01 level
Experimental	30	36.40	3.96	15.08	significant
Control	30	20.10	5.14		

The table indicates that the 't' value is significant at 0.01 level. Hence there is there is a significant difference between the two groups. As indicated by the mean value, it can be concluded that the students of the experimental group fared better in the achievement test than the students of the control group. This shows that learning with the help of blended learning programme will increase the achievement of the students better than learning through the conventional method.

Hypothesis 3: There is no significant difference between the pretest and posttest in the achievement of biology for the experimental group.

The 't' test applied to test the significance of difference between test scores of the pretest with that of the posttest for the experimental group.

Table - 3

Mean Achievement Test Scores of Pretest Compared with that of the Posttest for the Experimental Group

Groups	N	Mean	S.D	't' value	Level of Significance at 0.01 level
Experimental	30	20.43	2.07	20.52	Significant
Control	30	37.40	3.96		

Table 3 indicates that the‘t’ value is significant at 0.01 level. Hence, it could be concluded that there is a significant difference between the mean achievement test scores of the pretest and posttest for the experimental group. The higher mean value in the posttest shows that the students fared better in the posttest than in the pretest. This shows that the blended learning programme has helped the students to score more in the posttest.

Hypothesis 4: There is no significant difference between the pretest and posttest in the achievement of biology for the control group.

The ‘t’ test applied to test the significance of difference between the mean achievement test scores of the pretest with that of the posttest for the control group.

Table - 4

Mean Achievement Test Scores of Pretest Compared with that of the Posttest for the Control Group

Groups	N	Mean	S.D	‘t’ value	Level of Significance at 0.05 level
Experimental	30	19.76	1.87	0.034	Not significant
Control	30	20.00	5.06		

Table 4 indicates that the ‘t’ value is not significant at 0.05 level. Hence, it could be concluded that there is no significant difference between the mean achievement test scores of the pretest and posttest for the control group.

Findings of the Study

1. There is no significant difference between the experimental group and control group in the achievement of biology at pretest level.
2. There is a significant difference between the experimental group and control group in the achievement of biology at posttest level. The students leaning with the help of blended learning programme fared better in biology than in students learning through the conventional method.

3. There is a significant difference between the mean achievement test scores of the pretest and posttest for the experimental group. This shows that the blended learning programme has helped the students to score more marks in the posttest.
4. There is a significant difference between the mean achievement test scores of the pretest and posttest for the control group. This shows that the conventional method of teaching will not help the students to score more marks in the posttest.

Conclusion

In the field of education is not possible to equip the teaching leaning in higher and higher secondary level because most of the higher secondary schools suffering from lack of modern methods of teaching, they still follow the conventional method of teaching in higher secondary level. This should be change in the modern era; they should follow the blended learning methods in their teaching learning methods because it supports the education department well in advance.

Reference

1. Barbour Michael, et al, (2012), *Online and Blended Learning: A Survey of Policy and Practice of K-12 Schools Around the World*, available at http://www.inacol.org/cms/wpcontent/uploads/2012/11/iNACOL_IntnlReport2011.pdf
2. Rogers Carl (1983), *The Interpersonal Relationship in the Facilitation of Learning*, London: Rutledge
3. The Oxford Group (2013), *Blended Learning—Current Use, Challenges and Best Practices*, report 2013, available at http://www.kineo.com/m/0/blended-learning-report-202013.pdf (accessed July 2013)

5

Blended Learning for Future Generation

Introduction

Learning is a continuous process which exists from birth to death. An individual learns various facts things, concepts, events through various medium. Blended learning combines online with face-to-face learning. The goal of blended learning is to provide the most efficient and effective instruction experience by combining delivery modalities.

Blended learning opportunities incorporate both face-to-face and online learning opportunities. "The term blended learning is used to describe a solution that combines several different delivery methods, such as collaboration software, Web-based courses, EPSS (Electronic Performance Support System), and knowledge management practices. Blended learning also is used to describe learning that mixes various event-based activities, including face-to-face classrooms, live e-learning and self-paced instruction." By Purnima Valiathan.

Blended Education, Hybrid learning, flipping the classroom, whatever one chooses to call it, this method of learning–which combines classroom and online education–is going places and making headlines along the way. While education experts continue to debate the efficacy of hybrid learning, its very existence has challenged them to re-evaluate not just technology's place in (and out of) the classroom, but also how to reach and teach students more effectively.

Defining hybrid or blended education is a trickier task than one might think–opinions vary wildly on the matter. In a report on the merits and potential of blended education, the Sloan Consortium defined hybrid courses as those that "integrate online with traditional face-to-face class activities in a planned, pedagogically valuable manner." Educators probably disagree on what qualifies as "pedagogically valuable," but the essence is clear: Hybrid education uses online technology to not just supplement, but transform and improve the learning process.

That does not mean a professor can simply start a chat room or upload lecture videos and say he is leading a hybrid classroom. According to Education Elements, which develops hybrid learning technologies, successful blended learning occurs when technology and teaching inform each other: material becomes dynamic when it reaches students of varying learning styles. In other words, hybrid classrooms on the Internet can reach and engage students in a truly customizable way. In this scenario, online education is a game changer, not just a supplement for status quo. But what does this theoretical model actually look like in practice?

The strategy of blending online learning with school-based instruction is often utilized to accommodate students' diverse learning styles and to enable them to work before or after school in ways that are not possible with full-time conventional classroom instruction. Online learning has the potential to improve educational productivity by accelerating the rate of learning, taking advantage of learning time outside of school hours, reducing the cost of instructional materials, and better utilizing teacher time. These strategies can be particularly useful in rural areas where blended or online learning can help teachers and students in remote areas overcome distance.

Blended learning is a formal education program in which a student learns at least in part through online delivery of content and instruction with some element of student control over time, place, path or pace. While still attending a "brick-and-mortar" school structure, face-to-face classroom methods are combined with computer-mediated activities. Proponents of blending learning cite the opportunity for data collection and customization of instruction and assessment as two major benefits of this approach. Schools with blended learning models may also choose to reallocate resources to boost student achievement outcomes.

History of the Term

The concept of blended learning has been around for a long time, but its terminology was not firmly established until around the beginning of the 21st century. One of the earliest references to the term appears in a press release in 1999, when the Interactive Learning Centers, an Atlanta-based education business, announced its change of name to EPIC learning. The article mentions that "The Company currently operates 220 on-line courses, but will begin offering its Internet courseware using the company's Blended Learning methodology." The meaning of blended learning widely diverged to encompass a wide variety of synthesis in learning methods until 2006, when the first *Handbook of Blended Learning* by Bonk and Graham was published. In this publication Graham challenged the breadth and ambiguity of the term's definition, and defined 'blended learning systems' as learning systems that "combine face-to-face instruction with computer mediated instruction." Currently, use of the term *blended learning* mostly involves "combining Internet and digital media with established classroom forms that require the physical co-presence of teacher and students."

The terms "blended," "hybrid," "technology-mediated instruction," "web-enhanced instruction," and "mixed-mode instruction" are often used interchangeably in current research literature. However, recent researchers in the United States tend to use the term "blended learning" with more regularity.

Advantages

Blended learning is a formal education program in which a student learns – at least in part– through online delivery of instruction and content, with some element of student control over time, place, path and pace. Proponents of blended learning argue that by incorporating the "asynchronous Internet communication technology" into courses serves to "facilitate a simultaneous independent and collaborative learning experience", and this incorporation is a major contributor to student satisfaction and success in such courses. The use of information and communication technologies has been found to improve access to as well as student attitudes towards learning. By incorporating information technology into class projects, communication between lecturers and part-time students was improved, and students were able to better evaluate their understanding of course material via the use of "computer-based qualitative and quantitative assessment modules" in a study by Alexander and McKenzie (1998).

Why Blended?

Time: Defined opportunities and spaces for teachers to work with small groups of students to address learning goals (individualization), enhance or extend the curriculum (rigor), or spend time analyzing student data (monitoring).

Differentiated Experiences (Rotation Model): Face-to-Face Instruction, Independent & Collaborative Practice, and Online Curricula.

Personalized Learning for Students: Adaptive and assignable, online curricula individualize instructional pathways aligned with academic goals.

Digital Literacy: Reinforcement and application of National Educational Technology Standards.

Data to Inform Practice: Small Group Learning Stations provide multiple data points to measure student growth.

How Hybrid Classrooms Are Redefining Education

In a traditional classroom, instructors use class time to lecture and disseminate support materials. Students then review these materials and complete any assignments at home, on their own time. With some luck, teachers will review those assignments in class the following day, or at least host office hours so that they can field questions and offer support. “Flipping” defies these conventions. In this method, teachers and professors use online media to deliver notes, lectures and related course materials. Students review these materials at home and at their own pace. Classroom periods are then transformed into hands-on work periods where the teacher–who will have already delivered his or her lecture digitally–is free to field questions, engage class-wide discussions or offer other means of support. According to Mary Beth Hertz of the George Lucas Educational Foundation, “flipping” reinforces student-centered learning, allowing students to master content in an individual way. But is it effective?

Disadvantages

Blended learning has a strong dependence on the technical resources with which the blended learning experience is delivered—these tools need to be reliable, easy to use, and up to date in order for the use of the Internet to have a meaningful impact on the learning experience. Additionally, IT literacy can serve as a significant barrier for students attempting to get access to the course materials, making the availability of high quality technical support paramount.

It has been observed that the use of lecture recording technologies can result in students falling behind on the material in a study performed across four different universities, it was found that only half of the students watched the lecture videos on a regular basis, and nearly 40% of students watched several weeks worth of videos in one sitting. So we have to be very careful while implementing Blended Learning for our students.

Conclusion

“...Blended learning environments can create more and better opportunities for teacher collaboration, enable differentiated staffing and boost meaningful professional development opportunities...With sophisticated data systems, teachers have a flood of expanded and enhanced student data at their fingertips — improving efficiency and cutting down on time spent with routine tasks and record-keeping. Time saved from the thoughtful implementation of technology can be reinvested working with students, collaborating with other teachers and developing new roles...Truly understanding the potential of blended learning leads to the realization that teachers become even more important in a personalized learning environment."

Of course, no educational model is one-size-fits-all, and some hybrid classrooms are probably more effective than others. According to a scientific literature review published by the Australasian Society for Computers in Learning in Tertiary Education, a number of factors impact the success of hybrid learning. Teachers must be committed to and well trained in blended and hybrid education and its technologies, and students must have a clear understanding of what is expected of them in this new environment. As blended learning becomes more common, schools and professors will likely understand and implement it better. Yet even now, early in the game, blended education shows promise, making this an exciting time to be a student. Not all students learn the same way. This is not a particularly novel concept, but it is an important one. This is blended learning's real strength: it transforms a largely transmissive method of teaching–say, a professor lecturing for what feels like an eternity–into a truly interactive one. It sounds ideal on paper, but does it work? A 2010 meta-analysis published by the U.S. Department of Education suggests it does. According to the report, students exposed to both face-to-face and online education were more successful than students entirely in one camp or the other. Blended Learning is useful if we implement properly for the future generation.

Reference

1. http://www.grayharriman.com/blended_learning_articles.htm
2. http://www.grayharriman.com/blended_learning.htm
3. http://www.teachthought.com/blended-learning-2/the-definition-of-blended-learning/

6

Blended Learning – A Glance

Introduction

As of late there have been a lot of innovations and technological advancements that have transformed the educational landscape throughout the globe. The present "kids' society" is well aware of digital age. This is seen from the ways they use TV, Computers and other latest technological gadgets through Internet. They have to be capacitated in such a way they are to be treated as learning partners along with the teachers. It is necessary to look back (Past), look at (present) and look for(future) This will lead way to emerge partner institutions where the "Open educational resources " form knowledge bank. The erudition will be set off from different quarters of the world in which vocational and professional training will show resurgence. The teacher can never be replaced however new technological resources make an entry as the HUMAN teacher is only a natural resourceful and he can help the learners at all times. The innovations are the use of available resources at low cost but available to all anywhere in the world at click of a mouse through the computer. It is also a truth that the computer has become part of life like food, shelter and home. The latest information is art our door steps and so the present kids explore their power in a lot of creative way that ultimately the open resources of knowledge are made to go in air. This is definitely flying and the present kids and posterity are sure to use the knowledge with high quality couple with a way for further exploration of knowledge. It is clear that in this digital age many are very close with each other through mobile, internet, face book, twitter in addition to MOOC, Kahn Academy, blended learning, Edu Track and so on. This paper goes in to the details of building innovative society for posterity.

In general, it is considered that the humans are social beings or social animals. The present day education focuses on construction and development of innovation in the field of education for novel and creative society, producing productivity / produce, generating employability and increasing economy to the developing nation forever. The ever green Innovation is inevitable and unavoidable one in the present day society and the world. The Innovation is the indispensable in the nearby future needs and wants. It's certainly enlivens and enlightens the worldly or mundane things. Besides, it makes stuff cozy and comfort in the earth. Creativity is the hinge of the life and its part and parcel of the soul. Creativity has through its success, fame, name and process ever since the inception of the spices. It evolves from the Stone Age to digital and nano technology age. Blended Learning is a learning solution that uses a mixture of E learning and face to face instruction led courses.

Teaching and learning can nowadays become hi-tech phenomena. The teachers should possess soft skills and software knowledge to teach any subjects effectively and efficiently. The **chalk and talk** method is done away with mu CD and multimedia approach. The teacher should use advanced, latest, defined well designed recent method in the classrooms and it has become the conduit of the destiny. Among the various methods, the paper deals exclusively **"Blended Learning"**.the blended learning is the art or science or techniques, methods, or ways and means of the class room management for the purpose of learning.

Blended Learning means a solution that combines several different delivery methods, such as **collaboration software, web based** courses EPSS (***Electronic Performance Support System***) and knowledge management practices learning that mixes various event based activities including face to face class room , like e learning and self faced learning. Blended learning is a formal education program in which a learner learns at least in part through online delivery of content and in structure delivery of content and instructor with some element of student control over time, place path or pace. While still attending a **"brick and mortar"** school structure, face to face class room methods are combined with computer mediated activities.

The concepts of blended learning have been around for a longtime but its terminology was not firmly established until around the beginning of 21st century.

The term "blended", the hybrid", "technology mediated instruction", "Web Enhanced instruction" and mixed mode instruction are inter changeable transferable.

Meaning and definitions

Blended learning means many things to many people even within our relatively small online community. It is referred to as both Blended Learning and hybrid learning with little or no difference in the meaning of the term among most educators. Blended Learning integrates online with traditional face to face class room activities in a planned pedagogically valuable manner it is also defined a method of learning which uses a combination of different resources, especially a mixtures of class room session and online learning materials. In the fig 1 shows the position or status of blended learning with reference to distance learning and traditional method of class room learning.

Advantages of Blended Learning

1. Its facilities a simultaneous independent and collaborative learning experience.
2. It facilities greater student strength and greater faculty satisfaction.
3. It seems greater access to a range of appropriate, personalized and individualized learning teaching and resources.

4. It gives greater accommodation for learners and teachers.
5. It facilitates different age group, styles, expertise nationalities and cultures.
6. It fits different homes, workplaces, libraries etc
7. It promotes learning retention and transfer.

Blended Learning assessment

The levels of assessment of blended learning are as follows.

1. Knowledge
2. Comprehension
3. Application
4. Analysis
5. Synthesis

Blending Learning Ingredients

1. Line events
2. Self paced learning
3. Collaboration
4. Assessment
5. Performance support materials

Blended Learning is characterized by

1. Customization
2. Integration
3. Purpose
4. Flexibility

Blended Learning can be explained otherwise in the following flow chart

Access → Home/ Classroom / Workplace

Players → Instructors / Facilitators / tutor / Participant

Support Facility → Email / library/ training materials

Obstacles → Time / motivation / resources/ confidence/ support knowledge competency.

Conclusion

It is the compulsion of the time to have used blended learning for the present generation by the computer savvy teachers. By ignoring blended learning, no school/college/university could develop, improve the quality of education. Therefore, the state and the central governments, NGOs, higher learning institutes, human resources ministry, NCERT, UGC, NCTE, NAAC, SCERT, etc., will determine the usage of the blended learning in the present day generation with utmost care and interest.

74. Building Innovative Society for Posterity

7

Comparative Study of Effectiveness of Computer Assisted Instruction on Circulatory System For IX Standard Students

Introduction

This study investigated the compare effectiveness of computer-assisted instruction (CAI) and conventional teaching method in biology on senior high school students. A science class was selected in each of two randomly selected schools. The pre-test, post-test equivalent quasi experimental design was used. The students in the experimental group learned science concepts (circulatory system) through the CAI, whereas the students in the control group were taught the same concepts by the conventional approach. The conventional approach consisted of teaching, discussions and question and answer teaching methods. The students' pre-test and post-tests scores were subjected to Analysis of 't' Test, ANOVA. The results indicated that students that were instructed by the experimental group performed better on the post-test than those instructed by the conventional approach. This may help teachers in organizing meaningful teaching learning experiences and adopt innovative methods and approaches in teaching. Computer assisted Instruction (CAI) is a supplementary instructional strategy ineffective teaching. In this paper, researcher elaborates use, utility and importance of CAI in teaching-Learning. To create new approaches technique and appropriate digital learning environment applying in education for present and future generation. Based on the research findings recommendations were made on the need to develop relevant CAI packages for teaching-Learning biology in secondary schools.

Education should be an individual activity to a much greater content. Not at all children should be forced to go through the same steps of learning at the same speed. The high achievers will move faster in their learning where as the under achievers will need more time. Children have their own ways of learning. Some children may learn better through the use of different learning materials them by merely listening to an inspirational talk by the teacher. The style of learning may also change according to age. They use their season in acquiring knowledge. An important feature of education is its use of physical and intellectual tools. Education must reflect the influence of technology. This new technology demands new interpretations of the instructional process and those changed with educating the next generation must engage in a continual cycle of education and revaluation in the light of technological influence at all levels.

Education Technology

Educational technology is not a simple combination of these two words. It is usually thought of even more than the sum of the following two interpretations.

1. Technology in Educatione the effectiveness of the educatioal l combination or seperately bjective - vis-a
2. Technology of Education

Technology in Education

This is based on the application of engineering principle for developing electro mechanical equipment like motion pictures, tape – recorders, teaching machines, computers, television etc. This approach of education a technology is a bye product of the 21th century. Davis (1971) thinks that the hardware approach is based on the application of physical science to the education and training system which mechanics the process of teaching gradually so that teachers would be able to deal with more students resulting in less cost and economy in finances. It is said that good teachers have always used visual ads to assist their teaching ancient great masters used illustrations and models to increase the interests of their students. Today educational technology is stressing modern audio – visual and computer equipment.

Technology of Education

It refers to the study of principles and theories, formulate to solve problems in the teaching, learning process. The main frame work of education technology is provided by Technology or Education. 'Technology in Education' provides the support to implement the broader instructional design. It primarily implies systematic approach to instructional design incorporating alternative methodologies, media and aids with reference to the objective vis-à-vis learning content. This accommodates the systems approach, programmed learning etc.

According to the encyclopedia of education (1971. vol-9 P.22) Educational Technology is the purposeful combination or separately of objects, techniques, devices, events and relationships to increase the effectiveness of the educational process.

Application of Education Technology

Educational Technology has gradually influenced and developed the teaching learning process. Since the world is moving towards Technological growth information and special place in education. The trend is to introduce technological principles in the classroom. Educational technology consists of all modern media, methods and materials, which can be used to maximizing the learning experience of student at various levels.

Historical Perspective of Individual Instruction

The classical conditioning of PAVLOV opened a new chapter in teaching and learning and the behaviour gave importance to reinforcement as a major condition for learning. Edward Thorn dike improved the reinforcement procedure with stimulus (reinforce) response reaction, SKINNER (1967) expanded this idea as operative conditioning which led to the invention of teaching machine. Both kin aesthetic and information feedback are identified to play crucial role in skill learning by GAGNE (1963) LUMSDANOE (1964) proposed a new definition to instructional technique which was later applied in programmed instruction. The five golden rules applied in this preparation of programmed learning material (PLM) and the need for defining the objectives in behavioural terms in the preparation of instructional software material are proposed as essential by DANIEL DAVIS (1965). The three phases that help the teacher to decide in the ongoing focus on pedagogy are; what to teach (objectives) whom to teach (entering behaviour) and how to flash the procedures which are similar to the CAI model. FLANDERS' (1964) recommendation for interactivity in learning are subjoined through various learning activities built in the CAI package.

Individualized Instruction

Individualized instruction is the one-to-one relationship between a student and what he learns (DUNN and DUNN 1977). Individualized instruction is one of the most active areas in the education innovations. This kind of instruction helps the learner to learn at his own pace. Modern class rooms are characterized by a high degree of heterogeneity. Individual differences are pronounced among learners in large classes and to cater to the needs of the learners in such classes individualized instruction bodies is required.

Through individualized instruction materials self learning can be enhanced. This land of self learning helps the learners to learn even more difficult contents and learning of higher categories. Through self learning the needs and levels of the learners are considerably satisfied. The individual differences are considered and hence individualized instruction certainly leads to mastery level of learning.

Individualized instruction may be provided for the following reasons (DUNN and DUNN 1977)

(a) A gifted student, able to come with new consents or skills independently may work well ahead of his peers through the use of this method. He need not wait to learn until the teacher can work with him individually or the rest of his peers catch up with him.

(b) An interested student may learn more about a given topic, consent or skill after most of his peers have mastered it, may spend as much time as needed reinforcing the knowledge at his desire and pace until he too is ready to move ahead.

(c) An interested student may learn more about a given topic, consents or skill at the moment in time when he wants to, not when the teacher is able to get to the subject.

(d) An average student who cares to something new in an interesting way may become sufficiently motivated to work on his own because of the nature of the varied multi sensory experience.

Individualized instruction materials should have certain characteristics. According to MORE (1968), an individualized instructional material should have the following features. It should as

1. Permit the learners to explore freely.
2. Inform the learner about the consequence of his action.
3. Be self – pacing that is the student can more at his own rate of learning.
4. Permit the learner to make full use of his capacity for discovering relations of various kinds.

GOLDSCHMID (1973) maintain that any form of individualized instruction should possess the following characters. It should

1. Emphasize learning
2. Ensure active students participation
3. Stress evaluation and feed back
4. Principle of individual pacing

There are different forms of individualized instruction. Some of them are

1. Learning Module
2. Multimedia Package
3. Programmed Learning Material (PLM)
4. Personalized system of instruction (PSI)
5. Audio Tutorial Instruction (ATI)

Learning Module

A learning module is a short unit of instruction dealing with a single unit of subject matter self contained with define objectives. Based on the specified instructional objectives, questions are given and the learner assesses his/her performance in the subject.

Multimedia Package

A multimedia package consists of a collection of soft ware's of several media dealing with a specific topic on subject area and forming an integrated whole. Based on the interest and aptitude of the students, the students can select the media through which they want to learn the subject.

Programmed Learning Material (PLM)

Skinner has pronounced Programmed Learning Material (PLM) based on the theory of operant conditioning PLM consists of planned sequence of learning activity for achieving mastery in terms of stimulus response reinforcement relationship.

Personalized System of Instruction (PSI)

The Personalized System of Instruction refers to training which is based on self pacing and master learning. In PSI, learners work in their own and they must achieve mastery of a series of written learning unit. They are assisted by teachers and professors. It is possible to apply PSI.

Audio Tutorial Instruction (ATI)

Here the instructor's remarks, directions and interpretations of learning assignments and resources are given through audio cassettes. The cassettes are prepared by the concerned subject experts keeping in mind the target for which the cassette is prepared. Even for distance education system, audio cassettes are being used for instruction.

Computer Assisted Instruction (CAI)

The most exciting innovation in educational technology is the Computer Assisted Instruction (CAI). Though it was not skill developed like other individualized instructional materials, the day is not far off when it will revolutionize the whole process of instruction. **Taneja (1999)**

A computer is programmed with linear or branching programmes. It acts like a super teaching machine catering to the needs of a number of students at the same time. The characteristic aspects of the CAI is its capacity to initiate flexible instructional with the student. In this respect it is superior to the teaching machine. The computer can do this in different ways. The computer is able to record and store all the responses of all the students. It can use the information in deciding what information is to be given to the student next. It can branch not just in terms of on answer but also in terms of a whole series of previous answers. It can also record the time taken to answer a question and the decree of correctness of the student's response. It uses the information in planning to determine which branch or format would be conductive to a learner for effective instruction.

Computer Assisted Instruction is not merely a sophisticated type of programmed instruction but a different kind of instruction but a different kind of instruction altogether. No doubt, data processing, data communication, consents of audio-visual and media theory, communication theory, system theory and learning theory are annelid in the preparation of the CAI material. In contrast to CAI, Computer Managed Instruction (CMI) analysis the relationship between various factors concerned with the learning of a pupil and suggests activities appropriate to individual students.

Different Forms of Computer Assisted Instruction

Computer Assisted Instruction can be take any one of the following modes depending on the purpose of the material, the five different modes of CAI are

(a) Drill and Practice

(b) Tutorial Mode

(c) Simulation Mode

(d) Discovery Mode

(e) Gaming Mode

Tutorial Mode

In this mode information is presented in small units followed by a question. The student's response is analyzed by the computer and an appropriate feedback is provided. This is similar to programmed instruction. As in programmed instruction, the information may be given in a linear fashion as in branched pathways. The greater the number of alternative paths, more adaptive the tutorial can be to individuals.

Drill and Practice Mode

The learner, provided with a number of graded examples on the concepts and principles learnt earlier. The idea is to develop proficiency and fluency through doing all the correct responses are reinforced and the incorrect responses are diagnosed and corrected. The compute continues the drill and the learners continue his practice until mastery is achieved by the learner.

Simulation Mode

In this mode, the learners are presented with scheduled down stimulated. Situations bearing correspondence with real situation. Simulations are made to avoid risk, save money and conserve time, simulation of an aero plane in flight, an experiment on titration, a nuclear reaction, collision of two bodies are good examples of the simulation models in science.

Discovery Mode

The individual approach to teaching and learning is as followed. The learner is encouraged to proceed through trial and error approach i.e., by solving a given problem, realizing where and how he/she went wrong, trying again and finally solving the complex problem.

Gaming Mode

In this mode, the learner is engaged in playing opposite. The computer or opposite another learner. The extent of learning depends upon the type of the game. Games on spelling names of places and general knowledge are some examples of the gaming mode.

Information Handling

One area where processing and information handling capacity of computer is profitably used in counseling and guiding the computer stores complete cumulative records and match them against employment needs and potentialities as required for personal and vocational guidance.

Merits of Computer Assisted Instruction

Computer Assisted Instruction has several advantages over other systems of instructions.

1. Each student receives instruction at his own pace
2. Each student receives immediate feedback for his response
3. Each student responds continuously as he receives instruction
4. All units of learning are broke down into subunits and elements of learning in accordance with skinner's approach of teaching in small steps
5. Reinforcement of learning is achieved by personal message
6. Learning sessions are not manageable by designing the duration between half an hour to one hour
7. Student can access the computer any place
8. Students can learn in their own styles and ways
9. Students can test their own learning at any point of time to an end
10. Lesson from the theories of learning are taken into account at stage instructional design

11. Teacher's time is saved from the routine job of giving activity and employed in innovative instruction design and student guidance

Objectives of the Study

1. To understand about computer system and its working
2. To understand the educational application of computer
3. To develop scientific attitude among school students
4. To provide a broad – based biological knowledge, stimulate a deep interest in the natural world
5. To develop a CAI package for self instruction on the unit circulatory system in science for IX standard students
6. To enable the pupils to utilize effectively the instructional material in learning biology
7. To verify whether there is any difference in learning level between
   (a) Boys and Girls
   (b) Rural and Urban School
   (c) Government, Government Aided and Unaided Schools

Hypothesis

1. There is no significant difference between the pretest and posttest scores of government school pupils' following the Computer Assisted Instruction.
2. There is no significant difference between the pretest and posttest scores of Aided School Pupils' following the Computer Assisted Instruction.
3. There is no significant difference between the pretest and posttest scores of Unaided School Pupil following the Computer Assisted Instruction.
4. There is no significant difference between the pretest and posttest mean scores of the experimental group following Computer Assisted Instruction.

5. There is no significant difference in post test performance of Computer Assisted Instruction between the different types of school pupil.
6. There is no significant difference between the post test performance of Urban and Rural school pupil following Computer Assisted Instruction.
7. There is no significant difference between the post test performance of Boys and Girls following Computer Assisted Instruction.

Scope of the Study

1. The students can get more and adequate knowledge through self instruction material.

   It helps the students to develop self study habits, since individual study can be brought out with the help of self instruction material.
2. The study is expected to help the students at all levels, since computer plays a vital role in all the aspects of life especially in the field of education.
3. The present study is experimental study to compose the effectiveness of CAI and on "Circulatory System" for IX standard students.
4. In future instruction materials will act as a source of the knowledge for the teacher and students.
5. It will help the teacher in the teaching learning process, as it can draw the attention of the students by teaching learning computer.

Studies Conducted on CAI in India

In India at present several efforts are being taken up to develop the software for CAI, for individual instruction several studies also have been conducted to identify the effectiveness of CAI and Handout over the achievement of the students. SHARMA and GEORGE (1979) developed a CAI package of mathematics. Their objectives were to study the effectiveness of the CAI for school children and the findings revealed that the CAI packages produced significant result over the achievement of the children. BADRINATH (1986) conducted a study on developing and validating CAI package for reflection of light at the VIII standard level. He found that experience in CAI program appeared to be an effective method than the conventional method.

NACHIMUTHU (1988) has studied the development of CAI program on “Leaves”. He expressed in his thesis about the difficulties in programming a lesson. He also suggested that teaching will be more effective if the researcher himself programmed the lesson than using readymade diskettes. Because when the research programme, he can give all the points to be taught, as in conventional method and so the learners also will score marks up to the researchers' expectation.

PALANIAPPAN (1989) made a study on computers in education. He found that after introducing computers is schools for teaching, the attitude of teachers as well as students have changed. Many dull students scoreless through CAI, than the conventional method.

HEMALATHA (1989) studied on orientation of CAI. She concluded that the computers are commonly used in three main response sensitive strategies in CAI and suggested some levels of comparative involvement in decision making feature. They are drill and practice, tutorial and dialogue.

KARPAGA KUMARAVEL. R (1990) in his study on the effectiveness of computer assisted instruction video assisted instruction and conventional instruction in English language learning found that the achievement of video assisted instruction group in better than computer assisted instruction and conventional instructional group.

P. JEYAMANI (1991) pointed out that learning with computers offers a very powerful tool for educators and all efforts must be made to learners the potential of computers in education. This educational technology could therefore have a more on comparing role to play in the developing world. Thus the stimulation model of teaching through computer assisted instruction can readily be used for all types of teaching.

SARVANAN. M (1991) developed and validated a CAI package on X – rays for XI standard students. His findings revealed that the CAI packages were effective for individualized instruction.

PURUSHOTHAMAN and STELLA (1991) studied the effectiveness of CAI learning testing and guidance. The study reported that for low achievers self-testing and guidance through computer was found to be more effective.

BENEDICTO (1992) developed and validated a CAI packages on pollution for XI standard Biology students. The major findings of his study was learning the unit through CAI was faster for both slow and fast learners when compared with traditional teaching. He also reported the software developed ensures uniformity of achievement among Biology students.

MATHIVANAN (1994) attempted to develop and validate a CAI package on organisms an environment for IX standard pupils. His report revealed that the CAI package produced more significant effect on the achievement of the pupils of knowledge, comprehension, application and analysis level.

Dr. P. ANNARAJA and Smt. NIRMALA SUNDARARAJ (2005) made a study on power point presentation in teaching zoology pre post design was used in this that, they found that the power point presentation is effective in teaching zoology for higher secondary students.

JAYAKRUSHA CHOUDHARY (2005) conducted a study on effect of Computer Assisted Learning using method of enquiry in teaching physics in secondary school. Main objectives of this study was to test the efficiency of computer aided learning using method of inquiry in teaching physics at the secondary level on achievement and concept attainment. He found that CAI experimental method is to be more effective than conventional method of teaching.

G. SUBRAMANIAN (2006) pointed out major findings were computer assisted instruction significantly improves the performance of students, learning accountancy at higher secondary level. The combination of the colour, text, music and animation of the CAI package was well received by the students and the positive effect of same is perceptible from their achievement scores.

A computer factorial program on the laws and consents encountered in introductory physics courses among high school students was studied by EAUGHN AND KUHN (1979) these programmer were written with the weaker students in mind. But the researchers found that even stronger students used them presumably to check whether or not they really understood a particular phenomenon. This success was attributed to the fact that the programs were written so that each student's incorrect answer was dealt with in the novelty of using the computer encouraged students usage much more than the prospect of working from a study guide.

In another study, the efforts of CAI and reinforcement schedules on physics achievement towards physics of high school were measured by BANNET (1986). Seventy one high school students were taken as sample. The result of this study supported that students who received CAI would achieve significantly higher physics test scores.

PASCUAL (1993) conducted a twofold study. He applied linguistics approach and empirical study designed to measure the degree of motivation in students learning English using CAI material and Non CAI material. He found that students belonging to CAI material showed more motivation than their counterparts.

SIEGLE (2000) the purpose of this study was to investigate whether exposure to multimedia and presentation software on laptop computers influenced student achievement in a secondary level anatomy and physiology science course. The study demonstrated that students learned more when they had access to laptop computers, were exposed to multimedia software, and created projects with presentation software.

VENDLINSKI et al (2002) conducted a quasi-experimental study with 134 first-year high school chemistry students using the Interactive Multimedia Exercises computer based learning and assessment tool to solve qualitative chemistry problems. Results of this study show a strong and significant correlation between computer aided measures of student understanding and the teacher's manual evaluation of student understanding using her own rubric.

SUSAN et al (2003) in his study examined 165 teachers' beliefs about student centered learning as they implemented Alien Rescue, a computer based programme for middle school science that was designed to create a Student Centered Learning Environment (SCLE) in the class room. Discusses the goal of student activity, the role of the teacher, assessment, and student interaction.

RABIA TABASSUM (2004) conducted a study on effect of Computer Assisted Instruction CAI on the Secondary School Students Achievement in Science. In his study analysis of data revealed that the class IX standard students taught through computer assisted instruction as supplementary strategy performed significantly better. The CAI was found equally effective for both male and female students.

WINTERS et al (2005) in this study 62 high school biology students, paired heterogeneously based on prior knowledge, learned about genetic using Gen Scope, a Computer Based Learning Environment. The results of this naturalistic study could potentially be used to inform educational practice by highlighting scaffolds that may foster self-regulated learning in a CBLE mediated science inquiry context.

HARSKAMP et al (2005) conducted a study on solving Physics Problems with the help of Computer Assisted Instruction" In this study the main goal of most Physics text books is to develop declarative and procedural knowledge exercises provide pupils with opportunities to apply this knowledge. The computer group taking part in the experiment did achieve higher results in solving problems.

CEPNI et al (2006) pointed out that the study on effects of Computer Assisted Instruction Material related to photosynthesis topic on student cognitive development misconceptions and attitudes. This study result showed that using CAIM in teaching photo synthesis topic was very effective for students to reach comprehension and application levels of cognitive domain.

MAHAMOOD FARHADIAN (2007) in his research, he studied the co-operative learning, Computer Assisted Instruction and combination of these two methods called Co-operative Computer Assisted Instruction (CCAI). In CCAI method with the use of computer and attractive software, there would be appropriate grounds in instruction and educational achievement of mathematics for students. This method was examined for small group of student in a workshop. He had investigated some hypotheses on reduce of the students negative beliefs about mathematics, the speed of learning mathematics and its independence from time scheduling. Findings of the study, the difference between pretest and posttest scores were meaningfully significant.

Methodology

Educational software development and validation is a major research and development activity in the field of education. The major area in educational software is occupied by the instructional software development. The nature and the impact of computer and learning were led to its acquiring more significance. In the latest concept of improvement in the instructional software produced and the role played by educational technologists in the consents and process of software development. The CAI package depends on the electronic device. Further there is need for the subject export, technical expert. Individualized instruction is the one-to-one relationship between learners and the subject to be learnt.

Selection of Area

The investigator has selected six schools in Udumalpet at Tiruppur District which come under the Tamil Nadu State Board of Education. The sample selected for study consists of boys and girls from rural and urban schools.

Selection of the Sample

Sample selection is an important aspect of the research study, violation of a proper sampling method may yield based information of research and therefore maximum care is necessary for solution of sample.

English medium students of standard were selected from different types study the investigator selected three hundred students. Hundred and fifty boys and hundred and fifty girls of ninth standard from two government schools, two governments aided schools and two unaided schools have been selected.

Considering the non-feasibility of formulating randomized groups in a school setting, it was decided to have purposive sampling as the method of sampling for this experiment. Hundred and fifty students of Class IX in each of the three type of schools were taken as CAI experimental group and hundred and fifty students of

Hundred and fifty students of Class IX in different types of rural schools and hundred and fifty students of Class IX in different types of urban schools were taken as the experimental group. The same schools are brought under the categories, group of different variables are follow. Purposive sampling procedure is applied for selecting the sampling and so that it is free from any prejudice. The following table presents the details of the samples selected for the study.

Sampling Technique

For the present study purposive sampling method is used. The purposive sampling is selected by some arbitrary method because it is known to be representative of the total population. It is appropriate in a study which lays special emphasis on the control of certain specific variables.

Design of the Study

The design selected for the study is the pretest and posttest of two groups.

1. Administrating a pretest measuring the dependent variable at initial stage for elimination of novelty factor.
2. Applying the treatment to the subject, to measure treatment effect.
3. Administering a posttest again for measuring the impact of the dependent variable.

Differences attributed to application of the experimental treatment are then determined by comparing pretest and posttest scores.

Development of Instructional Materials

The subject is to be converted into CAI package was "Circulatory System" in biology for IX standard students. The content frame work of the syllabus was adapted from the prescribed text by the Tamil Nadu State Board Text Book for IX standard. The teaching points were collected from the text books and other reference books mentioned and sequence according to the designed learning level of students in the local school. The content prescribed was corrected into a reading material in simple language according to their vocabulary level.

The teaching frames were structured on the learning materials following the norms and theories set for the preparation of CAI package. The teaching points were structured in small dosage called "Frame". Frames were arranged in proper sequence. In each frame information was presented with simple illustration or examples.

Objectives Starting Phase

Bloom's Taxonomy was used for objective formation specific behavioral objective was formulated as performance objectives on completion of learning the unit "Circulatory System" the student should be able to identify. Content analysis was done. Care was taken to link the content by appropriate sequencing strategy.

1. Define "Blood"
2. State the composition of blood
3. Name the types of blood
4. List the properties of blood
5. Distinguish RBC, WBC and Platelet
6. Describe the functions of blood and
7. Define "Blood Group"

Description of the Tool Used

(a) *Computer Assisted Instruction Package*

The instructional soft ware package developed to help the learners through a prescribed form of self instruction the subject are to be converted into frame. In this study in biology CAI package was Circulatory System for IX standard students. This CAI package contains various stimuli such as showing pictures and animation. This CAI was an instructional effective material individualized.

(c) *Performa Sheet*

The investigator herself has developed a Performa sheet to collect necessary information regarding the individuals back ground such as the name, age, sex, name and address of the school, locality, type of school, system of school,

(d) *Science Achievement Test*

In this present study the investigator was prepared the achievement test question paper based on the IX standard State Board Syllabus. The question has been given to IX students of the selected school situated in and around Coimbatore. In consists of 40 questions and each objective has been provided 4 multiple choice from which the individual is asked to mark the response which he/ she feels to be right in their point of view.

(e) *Scoring Key*

The answer scripts for the conducted achievement test were collected and scored based on the scoring key. The score the test it was decided to give one mark as weight age for each correct answer. Thus a maximum of 40 marks who give correct response for all the items.

Jury Opinion

The copies of achievement test were submitted to a group of five subject experts who are teachers in schools and colleges for their valuable suggestion. Based on their ideas, the structure of questions was modified, options of some questions were changed and the number of question was also increased. They were asked to examine whether the items fully covered the content of "Circulating System" presented for IX standard by Tamil Nadu Text-book society. Items which were choose or similar or deviant was dropped as recommended by experts. They items reflected the entire context. Thus the context validity of the test was established based on expert judgments. As a result the test tool for the final study was prepared with forty multiple choice questions.

Pilot Study

Pilot study is a vital factor is any research. The pilot study administered to 50 student of IX standard level.

Administration of Tool

The study was conducted and materials were distributed to the students after taking prior permission from the head master of the selected schools. The investigator personally visited each school and collected the data. The purpose and intention of the study were briefly explained. The subjects had been repeatedly assured that they could freely express their opinions without and reservation since the purpose was purely educational research. The co-operation extended by the respondents/students was encouraging remarkable.

Methods of Experimentation

Each sample was pre-tested with criteria referenced test to measure the entry level. Before the experiment or treatment the students were pre-tested using the test. The test was helpful in accessing subject knowledge of the students prior to treatment. The same test was administered again after treatment effects. The individual instruction analysis was carried by employing't' test for difference between the CAI groups.

Data Collection

As presented pre test, post test was planned to achieve the objective of the study. The sample was selected for conducting the experiment. For conducting the experiment the investigator selected six Higher Secondary School, The investigator selected Higher Secondary School hence it would be easy to provide the treatment in the school to the sample.

Statistical Techniques Used in the Study

Appropriate statistical techniques were used which included the mean, standard deviation, t-test and ANOVA.

Analysis and Interpretation of the Data

Computation of Statistics

The first section deals with background information of the selected sample based on age, gender, type of school, educational status of parents, and socio-economic status of the family. In second section the scores of pre test and post test were calculated and the statistical techniques like mean, standard deviation, t-test and ANOVA were used for analyzing and interpreting.

Descriptive analysis for Background information of the selected sample

Differential Analysis

The collected data were consolidated, tabulated and analysed statistically by using the following tests.

1. **Test of Significance ('t' Test and ANOVA)**
2. **Mean and Standard Deviation**

(1) Test of significance: 't' Test and ANOVA

't' Test is used to find out the significant level of difference between two groups of population. The values are calculated with the help of the mean scores and standard deviation.

(2) Mean and Standard Deviation

Mean and standard deviation were done using the results of the study to make simple comparisons wherever necessary.

Analysis of 'T' Test Scores of Government Schools Pupil Following the Computer Assisted Instruction

Source	N	Mean	Standard Deviation	't' value
Pre test Score	50	14.300	3.2467	34.799 **
Post test Score	50	32.22	3.3030	

** Significant at 1% level.

There is no significant difference between the pretest and posttest scores of Government schools pupil following the Computer Assisted Instruction was rejected.

Analysis of 'T' Test Scores of Aided Schools Pupil Following the Computer Assisted Instruction

Source	N	Mean	Standard Deviation	't' value
Pre test Score	50	15.44	4.6342	22.206 **
Post test Score	50	29.76	4.3451	

** Significant at one percent level.

There is no significant difference between the pretest and posttest scores of Aided Schools Pupil following the Computer Assisted Instruction was rejected.

Analysis of 'T' Test Scores of Unaided Schools Pupil Following the Computer Assisted Instruction

Source	N	Mean	Standard Deviation	't' value
Pre test Score	50	13.16	3.6048	33.969 **
Post test Score	50	28.98	3.1975	

** Significant at 1% level.

There is no significant difference between the pretest and posttest scores of Unaided Schools Pupil following the Computer Assisted Instruction was rejected.

Significance of Difference between Pre and Post Tests Scores of Computer Assisted Instruction Group

Source	N	Mean	Standard Deviation	't' value
Pre test	150	14.30	3.9591	47.644 **
Post test	150	30.32	3.8831	

** Significant at 1% level.

There is no significant difference between the pretest and posttest mean scores of the experimental group following CAI was rejected.

Comparison of Posttest Performance of Computer Assisted Instruction Group between the Different Types of Schools

Type of the School	N	Mean	Standard Deviation	'F' value
Government School	50	32.22	3.3030	
Aided School	50	29.76	4.6451	12.824 **
Unaided School	50	30.32	3.1975	

** Significant at 1% level.

ANOVA test was applied and the calculated ANOVA value is 12.824, which is found to be significant at 0.01% level. There is no significant difference in posttest performance of Computer Assisted Instruction between the different types of schools pupil was rejected.

Comparison of the Post Test Performance of the Experimental Group Following the CAI with Reference to Locality

Area	N	Mean	Standard Deviation	't' value
Urban	75	32.00	3.2715	5.862 **
Rural	75	28.64	3.7331	

** Significant at 1% level.

There is no significance difference between posttest performance of Urban and Rural Schools Pupil following the Computer Assisted Instruction was rejected.

Comparison of the Posttest Performance of the Experimental Group following the CAI with Reference to Gender

Gender	N	Mean	Standard Deviation	't' value
Boys	75	29.6667	4.0415	2.084 **
Girls	75	30.9733	3.6279	

** Significant at 5% level.

There is no significance difference between the posttest performance of Boys and Girls following Computer Assisted Instruction was rejected.

Summary of the Study

The study is an attempt to find out, a comparative study of effectiveness of Computer Assisted Instruction and Handout Instruction on circulatory system for IX standard students.

A sample of 300 pupils studying in IX standard from six different schools in Udumalpet Taluk, Coimbatore District was selected. 150 formed of the 300 students experimental group following Computer Assisted Instruction. The experimental method was adopted in the study. Achievement test question paper was employed as a tool, at this time the treatment is administered on a small group of the target population. Pretest and post test are administered prior to starting and after the completion of the treatment respectively. The test scores were taken to assess the effectiveness of self learning through the Computer Assisted Instruction among students.

Findings of Study

1. The comparison of scores of pretest and post test of Government Schools Pupil following the Computer Assisted Instruction shows significant difference. The mean posttest scores is 32.22 for the Government Schools Pupil which is greater than pretest scores 14.30. This shows the Computer Assisted Instruction significantly influenced learning of pupil.
2. The mean posttest scores is 29.79 for the Aided Schools Pupil which is greater than pretest scores 15.44. This shows the CAI significantly influenced the learning of Aided Schools Pupil.
3. The mean posttest scores is 28.98 for unaided schools pupil which is higher than mean pretest scores 13.16. This shows the CAI significantly influenced the learning of unaided schools pupil.
4. The comparison of the scores of pretest and posttest of overall sample in target group following Computer Assisted instruction shows significant difference. This mean posttest scores is 30.32 for samples which is greater than the mean pretest scores 14.32. This shows CAI significantly influenced learning of all selected samples following CAI.

5. In this study it was found that same Government Schools has also showing better performance, while they received experimental treatment through CAI when compared to unaided schools and aided schools respectively in post test score.
6. The comparison of the posttest scores of urban and rural area in the CAI experimental group shows significant difference, the mean value of this CAI experimental group is 32.00 and 28.64 respectively.
7. Gender wise comparison in the CAI experimental group proved the significant. The calculated 't' value is 2.084. The mean scores of girls are 30.97, which is greater than the mean scores of boys 29.66 in the posttest performances.

Recommendation

1. Computer assisted instruction should be implemented in more number of the schools.
2. The Government should allot more funds to provide adequate number of computer materials for the schools.
3. It is recommended that Government may give concession for purchase of computer.
4. College students who are studying computer science may be asked to do projects in the development of necessary software for high school syllabus. This can solve the problem of non availability of software.
5. Special training shall be given to the teachers through in-service training programme to inculcate knowledge about different instructional strategies.
6. Educational institutions should have adequate instructional materials.
7. Training shall be given to the teachers to prepare and handle instrumental materials.
8. Instruction materials of learning provide scope for self instructional activities. Here the role of the teacher is limited and maximum activities are prescribed to the learners.

9. Teacher can improve their competence by attending in service training camps and also by writing research articles in the field of educational technology.
10. The students can learn effectively when they learn on their own. Self learning develops critical thinking in handling of study materials on one's own and enhances communication skills and self reliance.
11. The teachers must motivate the pupils to make more instructional package for self learning.

Suggestions for Further Research

A Research study would be incomplete if it doesn't provide necessary guidelines as well as potential research topics for further exploration. The following suggestions are made for further research in this area.

1. A similar study can be carried out in different types of school in different parts of Tamil Nadu.
2. In the present study researcher didn't take students from Tamil medium high schools students from such schools can be taken for further study.

Conclusion

The density of the country is destined in the classroom. Yes, it is true. The education has a wider meaning now-a-days. The education in the present trend does not mean the mere text book learning. It aims at giving complete life to the pupils. It is more important for the learners to know how to learn rather than what to learn.

From the results of the study, the investigator has ideas of Computer Assisted Instruction provided greater learning opportunities for children both theoretical and practical. Its use in bringing new kinds of experiences for children in school is really interesting and meaningful. The investigator therefore desires that the more number of educational institutions should come forward to make the learning best out of all available instruction materials for learning. So, this amount is just the beginning... not the end.

References

1. Aggarwal J.G (1995), Essential of Educational Technology; Teaching Leaning Innovations in Education New Delhi.
2. Bloom, Benjamin S (1956), Taxonomy of Educational Objective Hand books. The cognitive domain. Logmas Publication, New York.
3. Chauhan S.S (1983), Innovations in Teaching Learning Process, New Delhi. Coulson S.E (1962), Programmed Learning and Computer based instruction.
4. David Hawkeridge (1990), New information in Technology and Education, Croomhelm.
5. David Layton (1992), Innovations in Science and Technology Education, Edition III, UNESCO.
6. Ellington, Henry (1985), Producing teaching materials. A Hand book for Teachers and Trainers, London.
7. Forcier (2000) The Computer as a Productivity Tool in Education, Prentice Hall of India.Glass G.V (1970), Statistical method in Education and Psychology, Prentice Hall, Englewood Cliffs.
8. S.P.Gupta (1985), Statistic methods Sultan Chand & Sons Pub. New Delhi. Pp930.
9. Henry, Ellington, Percival, Fred and Race, Phil (2003), Hand book of Educational Technology, New Delhi. Hemalatha Parasnis, An Orientation to Computer Instruction Experiments in Education. July 1989.
10. John Best. W (1963), Research in Education Prentice Hall of India Private Limited, New Delhi.
11. Jaganath Mohanty, Modern Trends in Educational (2003).
12. Kothari C.R (1993), Research Methodology Methods and Techniques.
13. Krishnamoorthy. R (1995) Computer Programming, JJ Publishers, Madurai.

14. Kulkarni S.S (1986), Introduction to Educational Technology, New Delhi. Oxford, IBH Pub. Co.,
15. Mangal S.K (2000), Reversed Edition Foundation of Education Technology.
16. Murthy S.K (1995), Educational Technology Parkash Brothers, Jallandhar.
17. Narayana L.M, A text book of Chordates, Saras Publication, Nagercoil.
18. Palaniappan, V.P (1990), Effectiveness of Computer Assisted Instruction in Learning Triangles, Media and Technology for Human Resource Development.
19. Pillay, Subramania G (1995), Readings in Educational Technology, Nirmal Publication, Madurai.
20. Rajaraman, V (1985), Fundamentals of Computer, New Delhi, Prentice Hall of India Pvt. Ltd.,
21. Rao B, Anand and Ravishankar. S (1989), Reading in Educational Technology. Himalaya Publishing House, Bombay.
22. Romesh Verma, Suresh Sharma (1998), Modern Trends in Teaching Technology, Anmol Publications Pvt. Ltd., New Delhi.
23. Sadha and Singh (1982) Methodology of Educational Research, Prentice Hall of India.
24. Sampath and Pannerselvam (1994), Introduction to Educational Technology, Sterling Publishers, New Delhi.
25. Satyanarayana (1985), Research Methodology, Methods and Techniques, Atlantic Pub.
26. Vachan Sing (2005), Practical Approach Educational Technology, Akansha Publishing House, New Delhi.
27. S.Venkataian (2000), Encylopedio of Contemporary Education Series Science Education, Anmol Pub.
28. M.S.Yadav (2000), Modern method of teaching sciences, Anmol Publisher, Delhi.

29. S.M.Zaidi (2004), Modern method of teaching Science, Anmol Publisher, New Delhi.

Journals

30. Kiboss, et al JOURNAL OF EDUCATIONAL MULTIMEDIA HYPERMEDIA, Vol. 15, No.4, Pp 397-410, October 2006.

31. G.Subramanian, JOURNAL OF EDUCATIONAL RESEARCH & EXTENSION Vol. 43 (1), Pp 43, Jan-March 2006.

32. Cepni et al COMPUTERS AND EDUCATION, Vol. 46, No.2 Pp 192-205, Feb 2006.

33. Harskamp, INTERNATIONAL JOURNAL OF SCIENCE EDUCATION Vol.27, No.4, P 451-469, March 2005.

34. Roger (2005), JOURNAL OF EDUCATIONAL COMPUTING RESEARCH V 33, No.2, Pp 189-217.

35. Jayakrishna Choudhury, SCHOOL SCIENCE, June 2005, Pp 99.

36. Sharon et al (2005), JOURNAL OF COMPUTERS IN MATHEMATICS AND

37. SCIENCE TEACHING V 24, No.2, Pp 149-156.

38. Ndirangu et al, JOURNAL OF SCIENCE, EDUCATION AND TECHNOLOGY V 13, No.2, Pp 207-213, June 2004.

39. Chang. C.Y, JOURNAL OF COMPUTER ASSISTED LEARNING Vol. 20, No.1, P 4-10, Feb 2004.

40. Susan (2003), EDUCATION TECHNOLOGY RESEARCH AND DEVELOPMENT, Vol. 51, No. 2, Pp 57-76.

41. B.H. Helen Joy and L.SS. Manickam (2002), PERSPECTIVES IN EDUCATION, Vol. 18, No.4, Pp 235.

8

Focuses on Maximizing the Effectiveness of the Shared Resources

Introduction

Cloud computing in general can be portrayed as a synonym for distributed computing over a network, with the ability to run a program or application on many connected computers at the same time. It specifically refers to a computing hardware machine or group of computing hardware machines commonly referred as a server connected through a communication net work such as the Inernet, an intranet, a local area network or wide area network and individual users or user who have permission to access the server can use the server's processing power for their individual computing needs like to run a application, store data or any other computing need. Therefore, instead of using a personal computer every-time to run the application, the individual can now run the application from anywhere in the world, as the server provides the processing power to the application and the server is also connected to a network via internet or other connection platforms to be accessed from anywhere. All this has become possible due to increasing computer processing power available to humankind with decrease in cost as stated in.

In common usage, the term "the cloud" is essentially a metaphor for the Internet Marketers have further popularized the phrase "in the cloud" to refer to software, platforms and infrastructure that are sold "as a service", i.e. remotely through the Internet. Typically, the seller has actual energy-consuming servers which host products and services from a remote location, so end-users don't have to; they can simply log on to the network without installing anything. The major models of cloud computing service are known as software as a service, platform as a service, and infrastructure as a service. These cloud services may be offered in a public, private or hybrid network. IBM, Oracle Cloud Rack space, and Microsoft Azure are some well-known cloud vendors.

Network-based services, which appear to be provided by real server hardware and are in fact served up by virtual hardware simulated by software running on one or more real machines, is often called cloud computing. Such virtual servers do not physically exist and can therefore be moved around and scaled up or down on the fly without affecting the end user, somewhat like a cloud becoming larger or smaller without being a physical object.

Advantages

Cloud computing relies on sharing of resources to achieve coherence and economies of scale, similar to a utility over a network. At the foundation of cloud computing is the broader concept of converged infrastructure and shared services.

The cloud also focuses on maximizing the effectiveness of the shared resources. Cloud resources are usually not only shared by multiple users but are also dynamically reallocated per demand. This can work for allocating resources to users. For example, a cloud computer facility that serves European users during European business hours with a specific application (e.g., email) may reallocate the same resources to serve North American users during North America's business hours with a different application (e.g., a web server). This approach should maximize the use of computing power thus reducing environmental damage as well since less power, air conditioning, rack space, etc. are required for a variety of functions.

With cloud computing, multiple users can access a single server to retrieve and update their data without purchasing licenses for different applications.

Hosted

The term "cloud computing" is mostly used to sell hosted services in the sense of application service provisioning that run client server software at a remote location. Such services are given popular acronyms like 'SaaS' (Software as a Service), 'PaaS' (Platform as a Service), 'IaaS' (Infrastructure as a Service), 'HaaS' (Hardware as a Service) and finally 'EaaS' (Everything as a Service). End users access cloud-based applications through a web browser, thin client or mobile app while the business software and user's data are stored on servers at a remote location. Examples include Amazon Web Services and Google App engine, which allocate space for a user to deploy and manage software "in the cloud".

History

The underlying concept of computing dates back to the 1950s, when large-scale mainframe computers became available in academia and corporations, accessible via thin terminal computers , often referred to as "static terminals", because they were used for communications but had no internal processing capacities. To make more efficient use of costly mainframes, a practice evolved that allowed multiple users to share both the physical access to the computer from multiple terminals as well as the CPU time. This eliminated periods of inactivity on the mainframe and allowed for a greater return on the investment. The practice of sharing CPU time on a mainframe became known in the industry as time – sharing.

In the 1990s, telecommunications companies, who previously offered primarily dedicated point-to-point data circuits, began offering virtual private network (VPN) services with comparable quality of service, but at a lower cost. By switching traffic as they saw fit to balance server use, they could use overall network bandwidth more effectively. They began to use the cloud symbol to denote the demarcation point between what the providers was responsible for and what users were responsible for. Cloud computing extends this boundary to cover servers as well as the network infrastructure.

As computers became more prevalent, scientists and technologists explored ways to make large-scale computing power available to more users through time-sharing, experimenting with algorithms to provide the optimal use of the infrastructure, platform and applications which prioritized the CPU and efficiency for the end users.

Since 2000

After the dot- com bubble Amazon, played a key role in the development of cloud computing by modernizing their data centers, which, like most computer networks, were using as little as 10% of their capacity at any one time, just to leave room for occasional spikes. Having found that the new cloud architecture resulted in significant internal efficiency improvements whereby small, fast-moving "two-pizza teams" could add new features faster and more easily, Amazon initiated a new product development effort to provide cloud computing to external customers, and launched Amazon Web Serics (AWS) on a utility computing basis in 2006.

Growth and popularity

The development of the Internet from being document centric via semantic data towards more and more services was described as "dynamic web". This contribution focused in particular in the need for better meta-data able to describe not only implementation details but also conceptual details of model-based applications.

The present availability of high-capacity networks, low-cost computers and storage devices as well as the widespread adoption of hardware virtualization service – oriented architecture, and autonomic and utility computing have led to a growth in cloud computing.

Financials

Cloud vendors are experiencing growth rates of 50% per annum.

Origin of the term

The origin of the term *cloud computing* is unclear, although it is often attributed to the Internet Systems Division of Compaq

Computer. The expression *cloud* is commonly used in science to describe a large agglomeration of objects that visually appear from a distance as a cloud and describes any set of things whose details are not inspected further in a given context.

1. **Meteorology:** a weather cloud is an agglomeration.
2. **Mathematics:** a large number of points in a coordinate system in mathematics is seen as a point cloud;
3. **Astronomy:** a cloud of gas and particulate matter in space is known as a nebula (Latin for mist or cloud),
4. **Physics:** The indeterminate position of electrons around an atomic kernel appears like a cloud to a distant observer

Similar systems and concepts

Cloud Computing is the result of evolution and adoption of existing technologies and paradigms. The goal of cloud computing is to allow users to take beneût from all of these technologies, without the need for deep knowledge about or expertise with each one of them. Thc cloud aims to cut costs, and help the users focus on their core business instead of being impeded by IT obstacles.

The main enabling technology for cloud computing is Virtualization generalizes the physical infrastructure, which is the most rigid component, and makes it available as a soft component that is easy to use and manage. By doing so, virtualization provides the agility required to speed up IT operations, and reduces cost by increasing infrastructure utilization. On the other hand, autonomic computing automates the process through which the user can provision resources on- demand. By minimizing user involvement, automation speeds up the process and reduces the possibility of human errors.

1. Mainframe computer — Powerful computers used mainly by large organizations for critical applications, typically bulk data processing such as: census industry and consumer statistics; police and secret intelligence services; enterprise resource planning; and financial transaction processing.

2. Utility computing — The "packaging of computing resources, such as computation and storage, as a metered service similar to a traditional public utility, such as electricity."
3. Peer-to-peer — A distributed architecture without the need for central coordination. Participants are both suppliers and consumers of resources cloud gaming — Also known as on-demand gaming, is a way of delivering games to computers.

Service models

Cloud computing providers offer their services according to several fundamental models: infrastructure as a service (IaaS), platform as a service (PaaS), and software as a service (SaaS) where IaaS is the most basic and each higher model abstracts from the details of the lower models. Other key components in anything as a service (XaaS) are described in a comprehensive taxonomy model published in 2009, such as Strategy-as-a-Service, Collaboration-as-a-Service, Business Process-as-a-Service, Database-as-a-Service, etc.

Infrastructure as a service

IaaS-cloud providers supply these resources on-demand from their large pools installed in data centers for wide - area connectivity, customers can use either the Internet.

To deploy their applications, cloud users install operating-system images and their application software on the cloud infrastructure. In this model, the cloud user patches and maintains the operating systems and the application software. Cloud providers typically bill IaaS services on a utility computing basis cost reflect the amount of resources allocated and consumed. Cloud communications and cloud telephony, rather than replacing local computing infrastructure, replace local telecommunications infrastructure with Voice over IP and other off-site Internet services.

Platform as a service

In the PaaS models, cloud providers deliver a computing platform, typically including operating system, programming language execution environment, database, and web server. Application developers can develop and run their software solutions on a cloud platform without the cost and complexity of buying and managing the underlying hardware and software layers. With some PaaS offers like Windows Azure, the underlying computer and storage resources scale automatically to match application demand so that the cloud user does not have to allocate resources manually. The latter has also been proposed by an architecture aiming to facilitate real-time in cloud environments.

Software as a service

In the business model using software as a service, users are provided access to application software and databases. Cloud providers manage the infrastructure and platforms that run the applications. SaaS is sometimes referred to as "on-demand software" and is usually priced on a pay-per-use basis. SaaS providers generally price applications using a subscription fee.

In the SaaS model, cloud providers install and operate application software in the cloud and cloud users access the software from cloud clients. Cloud users do not manage the cloud infrastructure and platform where the application runs. This eliminates the need to install and run the application on the cloud user's own computers, which simplifies maintenance and support. Cloud applications are different from other applications in their scalability—which can be achieved by cloning tasks onto multiple virtual machines at run-time to meet changing work demand.

Cloud management

Legacy management infrastructures, which are based on the concept of dedicated system relationships and architecture constructs, are not well suited to cloud environments where instances are continually launched and decommissioned. Instead, the dynamic nature of cloud computing requires monitoring and management tools that are adaptable, extensible and customizable.

Cloud management challenges

Cloud computing presents a number of management challenges. Companies using public clouds do not have ownership of the equipment hosting the cloud environment, and because the environment is not contained within their own networks, public cloud customers do not have full visibility or control. Users of public cloud services must also integrate with an architecture defined by the cloud provider, using its specific parameters for working with cloud components. Integration includes tying into the cloud APIs for configuring IP addresses, subnets, firewalls and data service functions for storage. Because control of these functions is based on the cloud provider's infrastructure and services, public cloud users must integrate with the cloud infrastructure management.

Capacity management is a challenge for both public and private cloud environments because end users have the ability to deploy applications using self-service portals. Applications of all sizes may appear in the environment, consume an unpredictable amount of resources and then disappear at any time.

Cloud computing types

Controlled cloud services are not publicly available; users are specifically authorized by services vendors. Access to the controlled cloud may be through the Internet; however, connections would be encrypted. The cloud vendor employs various techniques and technologies to prevent unauthorized access. Use of services is governed by contracts, and which specify the responsibilities of the vendor and the responsibilities of the customer with regard to data

The services vendor discloses to customers its processes for managing customer data. Any sub processors used in processing customer data are identified to customers. Data protection schemes such as administrative controls, encryption methods, and other appropriate technical and organizational measures to protect data are described and demonstrated to customers.

Private cloud

Private cloud is cloud infrastructure operated solely for a single organization, whether managed internally or by a third-party and hosted internally or externally. Undertaking a private cloud project requires a significant level and degree of engagement to virtualize the business environment, and requires the organization to reevaluate decisions about existing resources. When done right, it can improve business, but every step in the project raises security issues that must be addressed to prevent serious vulnerabilities. Self-run data centers are generally capital intensive. They have a significant physical footprint, requiring allocations of space, hardware, and environmental controls.

Public cloud

A cloud is called a "public cloud" when the services are rendered over a network that is open for public use. Technically there may be little or no difference between public and private cloud architecture, however, security consideration may be substantially different for service that are made available by a service provider for a public audience and when communication is effected over a non-trusted network.

Hybrid cloud

Hybrid cloud is a composition of two or more clouds that remain distinct entities but are bound together, offering the benefits of multiple deployment models. Hybrid cloud can also mean the ability to connect collocation, managed and dedicated services with cloud resources.

Varied use cases for hybrid cloud composition exist. For example, an organization may store sensitive client data in house on a private cloud application, but interconnect that application to a billing application provided on a public cloud as a software service. This example of hybrid cloud extends the capabilities of the enterprise to deliver a specific business service through the addition of externally available public cloud services.

Cloud bursting is an application deployment model in which an application runs in a private cloud or data center and "bursts" to a public cloud when the demand for computing capacity increases. A primary advantage of cloud bursting and a hybrid cloud model is that an organization only pays for extra compute resources when they are needed.

Cloud management strategies

Public clouds are managed by public cloud service providers, which include the public cloud environment's servers, storage, networking and data center operations. Users of public cloud services can generally select from three basic categories:

1. **User self-provisioning:** Customers purchase cloud services directly from the provider, typically through a web form or console interface. The customer pays on a per-transaction basis.
2. **Advance provisioning:** Customers contract in advance a predetermined amount of resources, which are prepared in advance of service. The customer pays a flat fee or a monthly fee.
3. **Dynamic provisioning:** The provider allocates resources when the customer needs them, then decommissions them when they are no longer needed. The customer is charged on a pay-per-use basis.

Aspects of cloud management systems

A cloud management system is a combination of software and technologies designed to manage cloud environments. The industry has responded to the management challenges of cloud computing with cloud management systems. HP, Novell, Eucalyptus, Open Nebula, Citrix and are among the vendors that have management systems specifically for managing cloud environments.

At a minimum, a cloud management solution should be able to manage a pool of heterogeneous compute resources, provide access to end users, monitor security, manage resource allocation and manage tracking. For composite applications, cloud management solutions also encompass frameworks for workflow mapping and management.

Architecture

Cloud architecture, the systems architecture of the software systems involved in the delivery of cloud computing, typically involves multiple cloud components communicating with each other over a loose coupling mechanism such as a messaging queue. Elastic provision implies intelligence in the use of tight or loose coupling as applied to mechanisms such as these and others.

Cloud engineering

Cloud engineering is the application of engineering disciplines to cloud computing. It brings a systematic approach to the high-level concerns of commercialization, standardization, and governance in conceiving, developing, operating and maintaining cloud computing systems. It is a multidisciplinary method encompassing contributions from diverse areas such as systems, software, web, performance, information, security, platform, risk, and quality engineering.

Privacy solutions

Solutions to privacy in cloud computing include policy and legislation as well as end users' choices for how data is stored. The cloud service provider needs to establish clear and relevant policies that describe how the data of each cloud user will be accessed and used. Cloud service users can encrypt data that is processed or stored within the cloud to prevent unauthorized access.

Legal

As with other changes in the landscape of computing, certain legal issues arise with cloud computing, including trademark infringement, security concerns and sharing of proprietary data resources.

One important but not often mentioned problem with cloud computing is the problem of who is in "possession" of the data. If a cloud company is the possessor of the data, the possessor has certain legal rights. If the cloud company is the "custodian" of the data, then a different set of rights would apply. The next problem in the legalities of cloud computing is the problem of legal ownership of the data. Many Terms of Service agreements are silent on the question of ownership.

These legal issues are not confined to the time period in which the cloud-based application is actively being used. There must also be consideration for what happens when the provider-customer relationship ends. In most cases, this event will be addressed before an application is deployed to the cloud.

Security

The relative security of cloud computing services is a contentious issue that may be delaying its adoption. Physical control of the Private Cloud equipment is more secure than having the equipment off site and under someone else's control. Physical control and the ability to visually inspect data links and access ports is required in order to ensure data links are not compromised. Issues barring the adoption of cloud computing are due in large part to the private and public sectors' unease surrounding the external management of security-based services. It is the very nature of cloud computing-based services, private or public, that promote external management of provided services. This delivers great incentive to cloud computing service providers to prioritize building and maintaining strong management of secure services. Security issues have been categorized into sensitive data access, data segregation, privacy, bug exploitation, recovery, accountability, malicious insiders, management console security, account control, and multi-tenancy issues.

Cloud computing offers many benefits, but is vulnerable to threats. As cloud computing uses increase, it is likely that more criminals find new ways to exploit system vulnerabilities. Many underlying challenges and risks in cloud computing increase the threat of data compromise. To mitigate the threat, cloud computing stakeholders should invest heavily in risk assessment to ensure that the system encrypts to protect data, establishes trusted foundation to secure the platform and infrastructure, and builds higher assurance into auditing to strengthen compliance. Security concerns must be addressed to maintain trust in cloud computing technology.

Sustainability

Although cloud computing is often assumed to be a form of green computing, there is currently no way to measure how "green" computers are. Citing the servers' effects on the environmental effects of cloud computing, in areas where climate favors natural cooling and renewable electricity is readily available, the environmental effects will be more moderate. Thus countries with favorable conditions, such as Finland, Sweden and Switzerland, are trying to attract cloud computing data centers. Energy efficiency in cloud computing can result from energy-aware scheduling and server consolidation However, in the case of distributed clouds over data centers with different sources of energy including renewable energy, the use of energy efficiency reduction could result in a significant carbon footprint reduction.

Ambiguity of terminology

Outside of the information technology and software industry, the term "cloud" can be found to reference a wide range of services, some of which fall under the category of cloud computing, while others do not. The cloud is often used to refer to a product or service that is discovered, accessed and paid for over the Internet, but is not necessarily a computing resource. Examples of service that arc sometimes referred to as "the cloud" include, but are not limited to, crowd sourcing , cloud printing , crowd funding, cloud manufacturing.

Conclusion

According to Gartner's Hype cycle, Cloud computing has reached a maturity that leads it into a productive phase. This means that most of the main issues with Cloud computing have been addressed to a degree that Clouds have become interesting for full commercial exploitation. This however does not mean that all the problems listed above have actually been solved, only that the according risks can be tolerated to a certain degree. Cloud computing is therefore still as much a research topic, as it is a market offering.

In 2012 the European Commission has issued an analysis of the relevance of the open research issues for commercial stabilization in which various experts from industry and academia identify in particular the following major concerns:

1. Managing multitenancy at large scale and in heterogeneous environments.

2. Dynamic and seamless elasticity from in-house clouds to public clouds for unusual and infrequent requirements.
3. Data management in a cloud environment, taking the technical and legal constraints into consideration.

These findings have been refined into a research roadmap proposed by the Cloud Computing Expert Group on Research in December 2012 which tries to lay out a timeline for the identified research topics according to their commercial relevance. With the 8th Framework Programmes for Research and Technological Development the European Commission is trying to support the according research work along the lines of the Europe 2020 strategy.

References

1. "Cloud computing entry". NetLingo. Retrieved 15 January 2014.
2. University of Michigan. Retrieved 15 January 2014. Missing or empty.
3. "The NIST Definition of Cloud Computing". National Institute of Standards and Technology. Retrieved 24 July 2011.
4. "What is Cloud Computing?". *Amazon Web Services*. 2013-03-19. Retrieved 2013-03-20.
5. "Baburajan, Rajani, "The Rising Cloud Storage Market Opportunity Strengthens Vendors," infotech, August 24, 2011". It.tmcnet.com. 2011-8-24. Retrieved 2011-12-02.
6. Oestreich, Ken, (2010-11-15). "Converged Infrastructure". *CTO Forum*. Thectoforum.com. Retrieved 2011-12-02.
7. Dan Sullivan (2014-01-14). "Cost of the Cloud: A Developer's Guide to Reducing Your AWS Bill". Retrieved 2014-11-27.
8. Strachey, Christopher (June 1959). "Time Sharing in Large Fast Computers". *Proceedings of the International Conference on Information processing, UNESCO*. paper B.2.19: 336–341.
9. Simson Garfinkel (3 October 2011). "The Cloud Imperative". *Technology Review* (MIT). Retrieved 31 May 2013.

9

Access to Information As Long As An Electronic Device

Introduction

Cloud computing involves a large number of computers connected through a communication network. Under this, the three categories of services delivered are Iaas, Paas and Saas. Its characteristics include on-demand self-service, broad network access, resource pooling, rapid elasticity and measured service. It is highlighted by features like competitive pricing, object storage with a fully-featured API and flexible access. The various modes of cloud computing are public cloud, private cloud, community cloud, hybrid cloud and distributed cloud. The main enabling technology for cloud computing is virtualization. User self-provisioning, advance provisioning and dynamics provisioning are the cloud management strategies. Cloud computing is very useful as it is highly virtualized and organised in terms of portable workloads.

In computer networking, cloud computing is computing that involves a large number of computers connected through a communication network. In science, cloud computing is a synonym for distributed computing over a network, and means the ability to run a program or application on many connected computers at the same time. A model for delivering information technology services in which resources are retrieved from the internet through web-based tools and applications, rather than a direct connection to a server. Data and software packages are stored in servers. However, cloud computing structure allows access to information as long as an electronic device has access to the web. This type of system allows employees to work remotely.

Services

Cloud computing delivers hosted services over the Internet. These services are broadly divided into three categories.

1. Infrastructure-as-a-Service (IaaS)
2. Platform-as-a-Service (PaaS)
3. Software-as-a-Service (SaaS)

1. Infrastructure as a Service (IaaS)

It is also known as hardware as a service. It is a computing power that we can rent for a limited period of time. It allows existing applications to be run on a cloud supplier's hardware. Cloud provides offer computers – as physical or more often as virtual machines – raw (block) storage, firewalls, load balancers and networks.

2. Platform as a Service (PaaS)

It gives us nice API (Application Programming Interface) and takes care of the implementation. In the PaaS model, cloud providers deliver a computing platform and/or solution stack typically including operating system, programming language execution environment, database, and web server. It is a platform for developers to write and create their own SaaS (i.e. applications). It means rapid development at low cost. E.g. Salesforce.com, Windows Azure etc.

3. Platform as a Service (PaaS)

It is also known as on-demand Service. It is an application that can be accessed from anywhere on the world as long as we can have a computer with an internet connection. We can access this cloud hosted application without any additional hardware or software. E.g. G-mail, Yahoo mail, Hotmail etc., Also they can provide security features such as SSL encryption, a cryptographic protocol.

Hosted Services

The term "cloud computing" is mostly used to sell hosted services in the sense of application service provisioning that run client server software at a remote location. Such services are given popular acronyms like 'SaaS' (Software as a Service), 'PaaS' (Platform as a Service), 'IaaS' (Infrastructure as a Service), 'HaaS' (Hardware as a Service) and finally 'EaaS' (Everything as a Service). End users access cloud-based applications through a web browser, thin client or mobile app while the business software and user's data are stored on servers at a remote location. Examples include Amazon Web Services and Google App engine, which allocate space for a user to deploy and manage software "in the cloud".

Characteristics

1. On-demand self-service

A consumer can unilaterally provision computing capabilities, such as server time and network storage, as needed automatically without requiring human interaction with each service provider.

2. Broad network access

Capabilities are available over the network and accessed through standard mechanisms that promote use by heterogeneous thin or thick client platforms (e.g., mobile phones, tablets, laptops, and workstations).

3. Resource pooling

The provider's computing resources are pooled to serve multiple consumers using a multi-tenant model, with different physical and virtual resources dynamically assigned and reassigned according to consumer demand.

4. Rapid elasticity

Capabilities can be elastically provisioned and released, in some cases automatically, to scale rapidly outward and inward commensurate with demand. To the consumer, the capabilities available for provisioning often appear unlimited and can be appropriated in any quantity at any time.

5. Measured service

Cloud systems automatically control and optimize resource use by leveraging a metering capability at some level of abstraction appropriate to the type of service (e.g., storage, processing, bandwidth, and active user accounts). Resource usage can be monitored, controlled, and reported, providing transparency for both the provider and consumer of the utilized service.

Features

1. Secure and safe

Your data is protected through redundant storage at multiple physical locations. OAuth and granular access controls form strong, configurable security.

2. Competitive and flexible pricing

Choose a storage solution that fits the nature of your data, whether it's Standard Storage or Durable Reduced Availability (DRA) Storage. Like other Cloud Platform services, you pay just for what you use.

3. Object storage with a fully-featured API

Though Cloud Storage can be accessed with a simple API, advanced feature sets add flexibility and power. Object versioning, parallel uploads and CRC-based integrity checking give developers the ability to create robust, sophisticated applications. You can access the API using XML or JSON directly, or use libraries for several popular programming languages.

4. Flexible access

You can serve static objects directly from Cloud Storage or use it as a data store for other Google products. Access your storage from

BigQuery, App Engine, or other Cloud Platform services. Your data is accessible via an authenticated RESTful API that provides speed, flexibility, and OAuth-backed security.

Modes of Cloud

Public cloud

A cloud is called a "public cloud" when the services are rendered over a network that is open for public use. Technically there may be little or no difference between public and private cloud architecture, however, security consideration may be substantially different for services (applications, storage, and other resources) that are made available by a service provider for a public audience and when communication is effected over a non-trusted network.

The computing infrastructure is hosted by cloud vendor at the vendor's premises. It can be shared by various organizations.

Private cloud

Private cloud is cloud infrastructure operated solely for a single organization, whether managed internally or by a third-party and hosted internally or externally. Undertaking a private cloud project requires a significant level and degree of engagement to virtualize the business environment, and requires the organization to reevaluate decisions about existing resources.

The computing infrastructure is dedicated to a particular organization and not shared with other organizations. It is more expensive and more secure when compare to public cloud.

Community cloud

Community cloud shares infrastructure between several organizations from a specific community with common concerns (security, compliance, jurisdiction, etc.), whether managed internally or by a third-party and hosted internally or externally. The costs are spread over fewer users than a public cloud (but more than a private cloud), so only some of the cost savings potential of cloud computing are realized.

Hybrid cloud

Hybrid cloud is a composition of two or more clouds (private, community or public) that remain distinct entities but are bound together, offering the benefits of multiple deployment models. Hybrid cloud can also mean the ability to connect collocation, managed and/or dedicated services with cloud resources.

The organizations may host critical applications on private clouds where as relatively less security concerns on public cloud. The usage of both public and private together is called hybrid cloud.

Distributed cloud

Cloud computing can also be provided by a distributed set of machines that are running at different locations, while still connected to a single network or hub service.

Concept

The main enabling technology for cloud computing is virtualization. Virtualization generalizes the physical infrastructure, which is the most rigid component, and makes it available as a soft component that is easy to use and manage. By doing so, virtualization provides the agility required to speed up IT operations, and reduces cost by increasing infrastructure utilization. On the other hand, autonomic computing automates the process through which the user can provision resources on-demand. By minimizing user involvement, automation speeds up the process and reduces the possibility of human errors.

Users face difficult business problems every day. Cloud computing adopts concepts from Service-oriented Architecture (SOA) that can help the user break these problems into services that can be integrated to provide a solution. Cloud computing provides all of its resources as services, and makes use of the well-established standards and best practices gained in the domain of SOA to allow global and easy access to cloud services in a standardized way.

Cloud computing also leverages concepts from utility computing in order to provide metrics for the services used. Such metrics are at the core of the public cloud pay-per-use models. In addition, measured services are essential parts of the feedback loop in autonomic computing, allowing services to scale on-demand and to perform automatic failure recovery.

Cloud computing is a kind of grid computing; it has evolved by addressing the QoS (quality of service) and reliability problems. Cloud computing provides the tools and technologies to build data/compute intensive parallel applications with much more affordable prices compared to traditional parallel computing techniques.

Cloud computing shares characteristics with

- **Client–server model** — Client–server computing refers broadly to any distributed application that distinguishes between service providers (servers) and service requestors (clients).
- **Grid computing** — "A form of distributed and parallel computing, whereby a 'super and virtual computer' is composed of a cluster of networked, loosely coupled computers acting in concert to perform very large tasks."
- **Mainframe computer** — Powerful computers used mainly by large organizations for critical applications, typically bulk data processing such as: census; industry and consumer statistics; police and secret intelligence services; enterprise resource planning; and financial transaction processing.
- **Utility computing** — The "packaging of computing resources, such as computation and storage, as a metered service similar to a traditional public utility, such as electricity."
- **Peer-to-peer** — A distributed architecture without the need for central coordination. Participants are both suppliers and consumers of resources (in contrast to the traditional client–server model).
- **Cloud gaming** — Also known as on-demand gaming, is a way of delivering games to computers. Gaming data is stored in the provider's server, so that gaming is independent of client computers used to play the game. One such current example

would be a service by OnLive which allows users a certain space to save game data, and load games within the OnLive server.

Cloud management strategies

Public clouds are managed by public cloud service providers, which include the public cloud environment's servers, storage, and networking and data centre operations. Users of public cloud services can generally select from three basic categories.

- **User self-provisioning:** Customers purchase cloud services directly from the provider, typically through a web form or console interface. The customer pays on a per-transaction basis.
- **Advance provisioning:** Customers contract in advance a predetermined amount of resources, which are prepared in advance of service. The customer pays a flat fee or a monthly fee.
- **Dynamic provisioning:** The provider allocates resources when the customer needs them, then decommissions them when they are no longer needed. The customer is charged on a pay-per-use basis.

Managing a private cloud requires software tools to help create a virtualized pool of compute resources, provide a self-service portal for end users and handle security, resource allocation, tracking and billing. Management tools for private clouds tend to be service driven, as opposed to resource driven, because cloud environments are typically highly virtualized and organized in terms of portable workloads.

In hybrid cloud environments, compute, network and storage resources must be managed across multiple domains, so a good management strategy should start by defining what needs to be managed, and where and how to do it. Policies to help govern these domains should include configuration and installation of images, access control, and budgeting and reporting. Access control often includes the use of Single sign-on (SSO), in which a user logs in once and gains access to all systems without being prompted to log in again at each of them.

References

1. http://it.umich.edu/initiatives/cloud/content/what-cloud
2. http://www.crn.com/news/cloud/240150619/the-100-coolest-cloud-computing-vendors-of-2013.htm
3. https://cloudsecurityalliance.org/wpcontent/uploads/2011/11/DataCentricProtection_intheCloud.pdf
4. http://www.successfactors.com/en_us/download.html?a=/content/dam/successfactors/en_us/resources/white-papers/focus-on-cloud-security.pdf
5. http://blogs.gartner.com/thomas_bittman/2012/09/24/mind-the-gap-here-comes-hybrid-cloud/
6. http://www.morganstanley.com/views/perspectives/cloud_computing.pdf
7. http://www.cloudwave-f7.eu
8. http://www.irmosproject.eu

10

Designing Learning Environment of Tomorrow

Introduction

For today's children, technology is the part of their world. Technology is used to live, learn, work and play. Students have more access to technology than ever before including computers, smart phones, portable media players, e-reader and so on. As children are involved in using technology, we being their teachers have to implement innovative teaching strategies in the classroom. The content produced here is designing learning environment of tomorrow by making use of sophisticated technological instruments. The purpose of this paper is to know some of the innovations done in the field of education and also to know some of the learning environment such as web based learning, active learning classroom, m-learning, network learning, game based learning etc.

Change in education is the mother of all changes' because every component of life is influenced by education. Modern world has witnessed a change in its every sphere by the way of various revolutions like green revolution, industrial revolution and today the world is the spectator of another kind of revolution, the revolution in the field of information and communication in education. It is in the need that education has to address itself to this revolution which is fast taking place and engulfing every sphere of life. The learning environment aided by learning technologies is rich in evocative images and objects which trigger active learning by allowing students to engage with what appeals to them. The learner centered environment and visual situation provided by the display of students work in this digital era is important and display space is high priority for the learning environment for today and tomorrow.

Objectives for Designing Learning Environment of Tomorrow

1. Providing stress free learning environment.
2. Providing situation as per need and choice of the learner.
3. Providing freedom of pace, place and time for learning.
4. Giving less emphasis on exam oriented learning.
5. Providing child centered and activity oriented classroom.
6. Exploring children to the new learning theories which emphasis on creative and critical thinking skills.
7. Enriching and enhancing child's mental development.
8. Providing an opportunity for the learner with more flexibility in thinking.

Innovative Learning Environment of Tomorrow

Web- Based Learning

As a new delivering system, web based learning is a unique hypermedia instructional program which utilizes the World Wide Web (www) resources to create meaningful learning. One of the main features of wed based learning is that it allows learners flexibility to interact with each other at anytime and anywhere.

Web 2.0

'WEB 2.0 'is commonly associated with web development and web design that facilitates interactive information sharing, on the

World Wide Web. Examples of web 2.0 include web based communities, hosted services, web applications, social networking sites, video sharing sites, Wikies, blogs, mashups and folksomies. Web 2.0 site allows its users to interact with other users or to change web site contents, in contrast to non interactive web sites where users are limited to the passive viewing of information that is provided to them. Web 2.0 web site allows users to do more than just retrieve information. They can build on the interactive facilities of web 1.0 to provide network as platform, allowing users to run software applications entirely through the browsers. Users can own the data on a web 2.0 sites and exercise control over the data.

Web Conferencing

It is used to conduct live meetings, training or presentation via the Internet. In a web conferencing, each participant sits at his or her own computer and is connected to other participants via the Internet. This can be either downloaded applications on each of the attendee's computers or a web-based application where the attendee's access the meeting by clicking on a link distributed by e-mail (meeting invitation) to enter the conference.

Video Conferencing

Video conference might be regarded as the easiest and most effective web based collaboration tool in any instructional portfolio as they provide students with direct access to content, which is crucial in other collaborative project activities. Video conference provides students with the opportunity to learn by participating in two way communication forums. Furthermore, teachers and lecturers worldwide can be brought to remote or otherwise isolated educational facilities. Students from diverse communities and backgrounds can come together to learn about one another.

Active Learning Classrooms (ALC)

Active learning classrooms are spaces that are designed to support teaching and learning in an atmosphere conducive to engage students actively in their own learning environment. Active learning classrooms are mainly meant to engage students and promote active and collaborative learning. Active learning classrooms are designed to foster interactive flexible student centered learning experience and operate using central teaching stations and students provided laptops.

Blended Learning

It is the convergence of online and face to face education. Blended learning is replacing e- learning as the next big thing. Blended learning program are perhaps the highest impact, lowest cost way to drive major corporate initiatives. Blended Learning or mixed mode of learning or hybrid learning is the integration of face to face learning with online learning activities. It will be emerged as the predominant teaching model of future. Blended learning is many things to many people, even within our relatively small online learning community. In general Blended learning combines online delivery of educational content with the best features of the classroom interaction and online instruction to personalize learning, allow thoughtful reflection and differentiate instruction from student to student.

Cloud Computing

It is the provision of dynamically scalable and often virtualized resource service over the Internet. Users need not have knowledge of expertise in or control over the technology infrastructure in the "cloud" that supports them. Cloud computing services often provide common business applications online that are accessed from a web browser, while the software and data are stored on the servers. The technical definition of cloud computing is that " cloud computing is a model for enabling convenient, on demand network access to a shared pool of configurable computing resources (eg, networks , services, storage, application, and services) that can be rapidly provisioned and realized with minimal management effort or service provider interaction". This definition states that clouds have five essential characteristics: on-demand self service, broad network access, resource pooling, rapid elasticity and measured services.

Network Learning

Is a process of developing and maintaining connections with people with people and information, and communicating in such a way so as to support one another are learning? Network learning can be practiced in both formal and informal settings .In formal settings the learning achieved through networked communications is formally facilitated, assessed and/or recognized by an educational organization. In an informal setting, individuals maintain a learning network for their own interests for learning "on-the -job", or for research purpose

Virtual Learning Environment (VLE)

It is a software system designed to support teaching and learning in an educational settings , as distinct from the Managed Learning Environment.VLE will work over the internet and provide a collection of tools such as for assessment (particularly of types that can be marked automatically, such as the multiple choice), communication uploading of content, return of students work , peer Assessments , administration of student groups , collecting and organizing student grades, questionnaires, tracking tools etc. New features of these systems include wikis, blogs, and 3D virtual learning spaces. While originally created for distance education, VLE are now most often used to supplement traditional face to face classroom activities. These systems generally run on servers, to serve the course to students Multimedia and/or web pages.

List of virtual learning environment

1. wecCT – (Now a part of black board) software applications designed to enhance teaching and learning.
2. Desire2learn- Desire2learn eLearning solutions.
3. LAMS- the Learning Activity Management System.
4. eFront- an Open-source web based Learning management system.
5. Web train- Virtual live classes, enrollment, attendance, attention monitoring.
6. First class –messaging and communications solutions.

Pod Casting

Pod cast is the series of audio and video on the web that can be catalogue and automatically download. Pod casting is the method of publishing audio files to the web, which are then made available through subscription and automatically downloaded to our personal computer. One obvious use of pod casting in an educational contest is to create an archive of class lectures that students can listen to at their convenience. As pod casting is relatively new educators everywhere are still exploring the possibilities.

M-Learning

Mobile learning has different meanings for different communities. All though related E-learning and distance education, it is distinct in its focus on learning across context and learning with mobile devices. M-learning is convenient in the sense that it is accessible from virtually anywhere, which provides access to all the different learning materials available.

M-learning also brings strong portability by replacing books and notes with the small RAMs, filled with tailored learning content. Examples of M-learning are

1. In living
2. Mobile Bristol Toolkit
3. Savannah
4. Amicitias
5. My learning Author

Game Based Learning (GBL)

It's a branch of serious games that deals with applications that have defined learning outcomes. Generally they are designed in order to balance the subject matter with the game play and the ability of the player to retain and apply said subject matter to the real world. Children are allowed to express themselves as individual while learning and engaging in social issues. The success of the game based learning strategies owes to achieve active participation and interaction being at the center of the experience, and signals that current educational methods. Experience with and affinity for games as learning tools in an increasingly universal characteristic among those entering higher education and work force.

Examples of game based learning:

1. Global challenge Award
2. The New Media Consortium
3. EDUCAUSE learning initiative.

Conclusion

Thus we can conclude that the use of technology or the internet increases learner motivation and engagement enhances the change in learning style. It promotes the shift to a learner centered environment. Already wide spread in the school and colleges of developed countries. The new trends in education is also seen in India, which is slowly emerging, at the same time, there is some skepticism towards using technology in education because, impact on students achievements and cost effectiveness of what are often expensive applications are unclear. What is certain is that the mere presence of computer and internet facility in the class room is not sufficient. It needs to be designed and implemented strategically in order to be effective and line up to their full potential.

Reference

1. Khajaper. M (2001). The teacher education in 21st Century in India challenges ahead, Vol 39, No8, University of New Baroda, India.
2. Agarwal, A (2000) Web based learning and teaching technologies: Opportunities and challenges. Hesbay PA, Idea group publishing.
3. Pradeep Kumar T (2013) web based technology in education, First edition, APM Publication Corporation, New Delhi.
4. Patil Priyaj Murtuj, (2012) Internet in education. Edutrack Vol 11, No 5.

11

Study on Proactive Nature of Teachers of Ssc, Cbse, Icse and Igcse Towards Use of Technology to Meet the Challenges of Globalization

Introduction

Education is undergoing constant changes under the effects of globalization. The effects of globalization on education bring rapid developments in technology and Communication. These developments are bringing changes in learning systems and the roles performed by teachers. Unless the teachers, perceptions of their roles match with their role expectations, then only role performance matches the expectations. This study is to find the if perceptions of teachers regarding their roles and competencies are changing with that of changing scenario and whether the teachers from SSC, CBSE, IGCSE and ICSE are trying to be proactive to develop ICT competencies that are expected of them in a globalized world.

Teacher Education system is an important vehicle to improve the quality of school education. The revitalization and strengthening of a Teacher Education is a powerful means for the up-liftment of educational standards in the country. It inculcates the skills and competencies among the teachers and makes them professionally competent to meet the demands of the society.

An educational institution performs a significant function of providing learning experiences to lead their students from the darkness of ignorance to the light of knowledge. The key personnel in the institutions who play an important role to bring about this transformation are teachers. As stated by NCTE (1998) in Quality Concerns in Secondary Teacher Education. The teacher is the most important element in any educational program. It is the teacher who is mainly responsible for implementation of the educational process at any stage. This shows that it is imperative to invest in the preparation of teachers, so that the future of a nation is secure. The importance of competent teachers to the nation's school system can in no way be overemphasized. The National Curriculum Framework 2005 places demands and expectations on the teacher, which need to be addressed by both initial and continuing teacher education. Teacher education generally includes four elements: improving the general educational background of the trainee teachers; increasing their knowledge and understanding of the subjects they are to teach; pedagogy and understanding of children and learning; and the development of practical skills and competences.

Need of the Study

1. networking of educational efforts in secondary education will be a boon, especially to developing countries
2. pressure on the secondary education system for greater access and space for participation in Information and Communication Technology (ICT).
3. The challenge is to provide the young adults with the proper global competencies as well as appropriate environment and education management system that would foster networking among global educational institutions.
4. There is every reason to be proud of dreaming for better tomorrow and translating it into a reality.

Objectives of the Study

1. To study the proactiveness of teachers to meet the challenges of globalization in State Board secondary schools.
2. To study the proactiveness of teachers to meet the challenges of globalization in CBSE/ICSE secondary schools.
3. To study the proactiveness of teachers to meet the challenges of globalization in IGCSE/IB secondary schools.
4. To compare the proactiveness of teachers in State Board, CBSE/ICSE and IGCSE/IB Secondary Schools located in Mumbai to cope with the challenges posed to teaching profession as a result of globalization.

Design of the Study

Use of Descriptive survey of the comparative type. The comparative part of the study seeks to find out proactiveness of the teachers of the State Board, CBSE/ ICSE and IGCSE/IB Secondary Schools in using the Technology in effective teaching - learning process.

Sample of the Study

The sample of this study consists of 80 teachers (20 each) from International, National and State educational institutions in Mumbai. Stratified Random Sampling technique is used for selecting teachers from the schools.

Tools for Data Collection

Secondary School Teachers' Proactiveness Scale (an open ended questionnaire) is prepared by the researcher to assess the proactiveness of the teachers in the institutions of secondary schools.

Findings and Conclusions

The proactiveness of teachers towards purposes for which they are using computers is higher (90%) at the IGCSE board level schools as compared to SSC board (61.67%) where it is the least.

The proactive nature of teachers towards knowledge of Popular websites and purposes of visiting those websites is higher (80%) at the IGCSE and CBSE board's level schools as compared to SSC board (53.33%) where it is the least.

The proactiveness of teachers towards Networking with other institutions is higher (38.33%) at the IGCSE and ICSE Boards level schools as compared to CBSE board (16.67%) where it is the least. Overall, all the boards have given less importance in technological networking with each other institutions as revealed in the percentage terms which is below 50%.

The proactiveness of teachers towards using ICT to make teaching and learning effective is higher (65%) at the CBSE board level schools as compared to ICSE board (53.33%) where it is the least. The variance among the boards in percentage terms is minimum revealing that all boards are using ICT to certain extent.

Suggestions

Regarding the use of computers, websites, networking and ICT integrated class rooms,

1. SSC teachers require more practical experience and learning.
2. Teacher educators should concentrate in developing ICT skills
3. Still more student populations are in SSC boards than IGCSE boards. More attention needs to be given to SSC board teachers in developing ICT skills.
4. SSC board schools need better infra structural facilities for ICT
5. Proper training and evaluation is need of the hour for SSC teachers

Conclusion

Everyone wants teachers to use technology in the classroom. But you're busy — meeting standards, preparing students for tests — and maybe you're not too fond of computers, anyway. Never fear – there are easy ways to bring your classroom up-to-date, technologically. Now, as teacher educators, this is our dream and duty to make our student-teachers to prepare for global teachers.

References

1. Aggarwal, J.C. (2001). *Teacher and Education in a Developing Society.* New Delhi: Vikas Publishing House Pvt. Ltd.
2. Aggarwal, J.C. (2008). *Education in the Emerging Indian Society.* New Delhi: Shipra Publications.
3. Agrawal, Mamta, Jain, V.K. and Chandrasekhar, K. (2004). *Factors Influencing Effectiveness of Secondary Schools of Delhi.* Independent Study (DEME) NCERT. retrieved http://www.ncert.nic.in/publication/journals/pdf_files/indian_education_review/January_2011.pdf
4. Bates, Richard. (2008). *Teacher Education in a Global Context: Towards a Defensible Theory of Teacher Education. Journal of Education for Teaching, Volume 34, Issue 4, pages 277 - 293* retrieved from http://hdl.handle.net/10536/DRO/DU:30017494
5. Best, J.W., and Kahn, J.V. (2005). *Research in Education.* New Delhi: Pearson education, Inc. Pearson Prentice Hall.
6. Eric, B. (2003). *Globalization and Higher Education Research.* DOI: 10.1177/1028315303007002002, Journal of Studies in International Education, vol. 7 no. 2. 128-148
7. Experiment-Resources.com (2008). Statistics Tutorial. Retrieved 16 Jul. 2011 from Experiment Resources: http://www.experiment-resources.com/statistics-tutorial.html
8. ICSE School Boards retrieved from http://www.cisce.org/ICSE%20SYLLABUSES%202012%20FINAL%20CRC/1.Syllabus%20Regulations.pdf
9. ICFAI Center for Management Research (2005). *Business Research Methods.* Hyderabad.
10. IGCSE school Boards retrieved from http://www.cie.org.uk/
11. *Karaman, K. (2010). Globalization and Education.* Journal: Zeitschrift für die Welt der Türken, Vol: 2 Issue: 3 Pages/record No.: 131- 144 http://www.doaj.org/doaj?func=abstract&id=664796
12. Kelly, A. (2009).*Globalization and Education: A Review of Conflicting Perspectives and their Effect on Policy and*

Professional Practice in the UK." #EJ827822, *Globalization* Societies and Education, v7 n1 p51-68 retrieved from http://www.tandfonline.com/doi/abs/10.1080/14767720802677333

13. Kothari. C. R. (2006). *Research Methodology, Methods & Techniques.* Delhi: New Age International Publishers.
14. Koul,L.(2007). *Methodology of Educational Research.* Delhi: Vikas Publishing House Pvt Ltd.
15. NIEPA, (2003) *Globalization and Challenges for Education.* New Delhi: Shipra Publications.
16. One -way ANOVA. (2012) Retrieved from http://www.gs.washington.edu/academics/courses/akey/.../lecture7.pdf
17. Pandey V.C (2004) *Digital Technologies and Teaching Strategies.* New Delhi: Isha Books.
18. Taylor and Francis Group (2007).*Globalization, Societies and Education.* ISSN 1476-7724, Online ISSN: 1476-7732 Published By: Routledge, Volume Number: 9
19. t-TEST. Retrieved from http://stattrek.com/hypothesis-test/difference-in-means.aspx
20. t-TEST. Retrieved from http://www.indiana.edu/~educy520/sec6342/week_10/ttest_exp.pdf
21. Von Hippel, Paul T. (2005), *Mean, Median, and Skew: Correcting a Textbook Rule :* Journal of Statistics Education 13 (2). Volume 13, Number 2 (2005), www.amstat.org/publications/jse/v13n2/vonhippel.html
22. Walia J.S (2005). *Principles and Methods of Education.* Punjab: Paul Publishers. Wakefield, Peter, Pumfrey, D.(2009). *Illuminating and Improving National curriculum Development: Students' Perceptions and Suggestions. A Pilot Study in a State Secondary school;* EJ833063 Educational Review, v61 n1 p63-83 http://www.ingentaconnect.com/content/routledg/cedr/2009/00000061/00000001/art00004

12

Building Innovations for Creative Society and Generating Employability –Beyond Digital Age

Introduction

Blended learning is a new educational model with great potential to increase student outcomes and create exciting new roles for teachers. In this course you will learn about the different types of blended learning and the best practices from real schools using these models. Blended courses integrate face-to-face and online learning. Online and classroom activities and course materials are selected to complement each other, to engage students and to achieve specified learning outcomes. In this paper I would like to explore the different models of blended learning and how blended learning will help the students for self learning. This is the best technique applying in education for present and future generation.

Blended learning is a new educational model with great potential to increase student outcomes and create exciting new roles for teachers. In this course you will learn about the different types of blended learning and the best practices from real schools using these models. In addition, you will develop the tools you need to build your own blended learning program.

This course is designed for anyone with a strong interest in blended learning. We anticipate participation from educators as well as parents and members of the education technology sector, philanthropy, non-profits, etc. That said, it is ideal to have some access to some form of a classroom (a friend, colleague, after school program, etc.) to take the most advantage of the course because we strongly believe in people being able to try out these ideas. That said, there are pathways in the course for people who have access to a classroom and those who do not.

Defining Blended Learning

For years now, the term "Blended Learning" has been used to describe a sort of middle ground between face-to-face and fully online education. I wanted to explore several of these evolving definitions. Here are a few that stand out to me:

The Clayton Christensen Institute created one of the most commonly accepted definitions: "A formal education program in which a student learns

1. At part through online learning, with some element of student control over time, place, path, and/or pace;
2. At least in part in a supervised brick-and-mortar location away from home;
3. And the modalities along each student's learning path within a course or subject are connected to provide an integrated learning experience."

The Sloan Consortium has define Blended Learning as "instruction that has between 30 and 80 percent of the course content delivered online," as contrasted with online courses, in which 80 percent is delivered online, and face-to-face instruction, in which zero to 29 percent of the content is delivered online. I think all of these definitions true in different ways. So, I thought, *"Blended learning combines face-to-face interaction with a teacher in a brick-and-mortar school location, with additional instruction— whether live* *and or recorded– conducted in an online learning environment that allows for digital content, personalized learning, and collaboration with fellow students."*

Purpose of Blended Learning

A critical element to the blended learning concept is reduced seat time. Reduction of time that students spend in a face-to-face, traditional classroom format serves several purposes that offer several benefits including:

(1) Institutions have the potential to manage instructional and facility resources more efficiently, teaching more students within a semester.

(2) This approach is beneficial for students, providing the convenience and flexibility associated with online learning, freeing up time for work, family obligations or extra-curricular activities.

(3) Blended learning develops a skill set for students that otherwise would not be possible in exclusive face-to-face instruction. Skills include digital citizenship, information management skills, self-directed learning, and web research and collaboration skills.

About the Course

Plenty of buzz exists about blended learning and its transformational potential. In this course we will explore the different models of blended learning and dive into key issues that impact students, teachers, and schools. Specifically, we will look at these issues through the lens of three high-performing schools that each uses a different type of blended learning. A few of the key topics will include:

- The role of the student and how to support students in the transition from traditional to blended learning
- Implications for teachers in their day-to-day work and overall role

- Impact on the way schools are designed including staffing models, use of time, hardware/software selection, and the use of data
- Implementation challenges, potential solutions, and the remaining open questions

We will live by the attributes of blended learning in this course, encouraging students to take quizzes at the beginning of the week to assess their understanding and skip material they already know. In addition, the course will culminate in participant's prototyping their own blended learning model and will have an overall hands-on approach.

If you are interested in learning more about how to best leverage technology in education and rethink the way we run schools, join this MOOC and encourage your colleagues to do the same. Become a part of this growing movement and learn first-hand Blended learning is a new educational model with great potential to increase student outcomes and create exciting new roles for teachers. In this course you will learn about the different types of blended learning and the best practices from real schools using these models Consider signing up for the signature track so you can have a verified certificate of your completion of this course.

Course Syllabus

"Blended Learning: Personalizing Education for Students" explores Blended learning is a new educational model with great potential to increase student outcomes and create exciting new roles for teachers. In this course you will learn about the different types of blended learning and the best practices from real schools using these models the topics covered in the course include:

1. The definition of blended learning and several blended learning models
2. The role of the student and how to support students in the transition from traditional to blended learning
3. The role of the teacher and blended learning's implications for teachers in their day-to-day work and overall role

4. The impact of blended learning on the way schools are designed including staffing models and use of time
5. The selection of appropriate hardware and software in blended learning models and the use of space and the design of facilities
6. A process for innovation and continuous improvement in blended learning models

Advantages of Blended Learning

Blended courses integrate face-to-face and online learning. Online and classroom activities and course materials are selected to complement each other, to engage students and to achieve specified learning outcomes. Many instructors favour blended learning because it can:

1. increase the amount and quality of faculty-to-student and student-to-student interaction;
2. increase opportunities for active and collaborative learning and assessment before, during and after lectures;
3. help students prepare for class discussions or lab work;
4. facilitate more varied and engaging media for presenting course content;
5. address learning bottlenecks via new types of interactive and independent learning activities;
6. allow class time to be spent on active learning activities by shifting background or foundational content to the online environment;
7. help to create a sense of community in large classes;
8. Allow students to access course materials when and where they want, at their own pace.

Blended courses do not follow a single formula. Some use the online environment for content or lecture delivery and the classroom for active learning opportunities, whereas others use the face-to-face time for lectures and the online environment for discussions, assessments or other learning activities. Some use a combination of these two approaches and employ the "flipped classroom".

In a flipped classroom lectures or other materials are delivered online for some classes or tutorials and students use these materials to prepare for active learning in the classroom. The in-class activities often involve peer learning or small group activities to engage students in discussion or problem solving.

- Support for blended learning,
- *Senior Instructional Developer, Blended Learning*
- *Centre for Teaching Excellence faculty liaisons*
- *Teaching Excellence Academy*
- *Instructor resource repository*
- *Teaching assistant training*
- *Assessing the impact of your blended course*

Conclusion

A blended program can be the best of both worlds, and though a significant undertaking, once implemented successfully, such a program has significant benefits for the institution *and* students. Students embrace flexibility, embrace being in a connected world that the web provides, it's no wonder that blended programs rank high in learning outcomes and satisfaction. Blended learning programs truly are the best of both worlds for students, instructors and the institution.

References

1. Blended Learning (2004), Dziuban, Hartman J. and Moskal P., EDUCAUSE Center for Applied Research
2. Enhancing Student Learning and Retention with Blended Learning Class Guides (2010) Amaral & Shank
3. Preparing the Academy of Today for the Learner Tomorrow (2007), Dziuban, Hartman J. and Moskal P
4. Blended Learning in K-12, Innosight Institute

5. *Can College Students Have it All? Learn when and where they want?* Online Learning Insights

6. *California to Give Web Courses a Big Trial* (2012), Lewin & Markoff, New York Times

13

Designing Learning Environment of Tomorrow- School Facilities that Support the User

Introduction

This paper presents the conclusions of a study, carried out in collaboration with schools in six European countries, which focused on tomorrow's physical learning environments. It resulted in the creation of a learning space model that is flexible, modifiable and sustainable while supporting the teaching and learning processes. It is widely acknowledged amongst today's educators that teachers' roles have changed dramatically since the last century.

In recent years, we have witnessed rapid social and cultural changes, phenomenal advances in communication and information technologies, as well as the introduction of the Internet within schools. These factors have contributed to shape the teaching and operating cultures of schools and created shifts in our expectations of the physical learning environment. They have affected teachers, educators and researchers the world over. These miniature revolutions have given rise to an urgent need for a new generation of facilities to cater for 21st century teaching and learning needs.

Conceptualizing the physical learning Environment

The concept of "learning environment" will become increasingly significant as schools of the future become centers of lifelong learning. "Learning environment" is a term used liberally in educational discourse because of the emerging use of information technologies for educational purposes on the one hand, and the constructivist concept of knowledge and learning on the other (Mononen-Aaltonen, 1998).

The OECD (2006) defines "educational spaces" as "a physical space that supports multiple and diverse teaching and learning programmes and pedagogies, including current technologies; one that demonstrates optimal, cost-effective building performance and operation over time; one that respects and is in harmony with the environment; and one that encourages social participation, providing a healthy, comfortable, safe, secure and stimulating setting for its occupants".

In its narrowest sense, a physical learning environment is seen as a conventional classroom and, in its widest sense, as a combination of formal and informal education systems where learning takes place both inside and outside of schools (Manninen et al., 2007). Manninen criticized traditional school teaching for conveying too much theoretical information and for preventing in-depth learning. He claims that inert knowledge is relevant for exams but not for real-world problems. This idea is posing new challenges and exerting pressure to bring about changes in physical learning environments.

The concept of the physical learning environment with respect to physical structures relates to spaces, equipment and tools within the school. Lehtinen (1997, p. 21) suggests that the concept has evolved into an even more complex structure that includes teaching equipment, sources of information and events outside of schools, where students can take part in the learning process both directly and virtually. The term evolved as a result of the recent changes taking place in pedagogy, whereby actual learning has been transposed outside of schools thanks to developments in communication and information technology.

Internet has already brought about significant changes in schools. Both the immense quantity of information available and easy access to social networks have weakened the link between schools and learning and therefore modified the traditional teacher-student scenario. The learning process is becoming more co-operative, changing the teacher into a learner too. Manninen (2007, p. 27) categorizes learning according to five different contexts: physical, local, social, technological and didactic. The basic structure of teaching spaces does not seem to have evolved much over the past century. This fact inspired the research team to investigate the reason why, despite the recent changes in pedagogy and the widespread use of information technology inside classrooms and school spaces, the physical learning environment has not yet changed in keeping with this evolution.

In order to plan and construct effective physical learning environments, not only technical specifications need to be elaborated; qualitative aspects also need to be considered (Nuikkinen 2009, p. 64). The concept of "quality design" has become critical the world over. It relates to school construction and, more particularly, defining a quality physical learning environment, measuring it and analyzing the results (OECD, 2006). With regard to quality criteria for school building and design, the key actors are students; requirements are determined by specific age groups, in conjunction with societal needs and regulations relating to usability and safety (Heitor, 2005). It has been demonstrated that international comparisons of education can be achieved through comprehensive quality management and quality criteria (Finnish National Board of Education, 2008; OECD, 2006). As a result, the emphasis is shifting from developing physical learning environments using norms and regulations to comparing these environments on the basis of qualitative improvement (OECD, 2009).

Objectives of the Study

With these considerations in mind, a comprehensive study was undertaken of what composes a physical learning environment. This would seem to consist of four learning contexts: social, individual, formal teaching and informal learning processes. These elements form an interactive whole in which the physical learning environment plays a central role in reforming the school's operational culture; it should be analyzed and developed holistically. This study approaches the subject by considering the learning space and its operational environment as such. Within it, flexible and modifiable learning spaces and their related learning environments are formed through pairs of dimensions. They are all interactive and totally supportive of one another, as shown below

Supportive learning contents

The study took place between 2007 and 2010. Its objective, which was to contribute to the quality of education, arose from concerns shared by groups of students, teachers and educational administrators about the changes which needed to be implemented in physical learning environments. A school from each of the following countries – Belgium, Finland, Holland, Portugal, Spain and Sweden – participated in the study. They all shared common features such as infrastructure, educational level and socio- economic conditions. The study set out to conceptualize the relationship between educations, the physical learning environment and the facilities needed by its users.

Participants were asked to identify the components that make up good qualitative and modifiable learning spaces: it was commonly agreed that improving educational facilities was key in this regard. It attempted to highlight the qualitative factors and user-oriented design features of physical learning environments. When comparing international physical learning environment criteria and their associate recommendations, we found that expectations relating to changeability, flexibility and sustainability were key factors.

Implementing the Study

Information on users' and school authorities' perceptions was collected from the six countries using different methods: 250 14- and 15-year-old students from the six participating countries were invited to design their ideal model classroom, using a 1:50 scale and including a specific set of furniture and equipment. Students were asked to arrange the furniture to suit their learning needs and according to how they would like tomorrow's classroom to be configured; they were also asked to suggest alternative space solutions. In addition, 65 teachers completed questionnaires and 35 administrative school authorities were interviewed.

We therefore used process simulation, which is a targeted research method used in specific circumstances such as when the physical learning environment is inspected through a co-operative design process (Smeds et al., 2007). This method has been used in Finland to plan large-scale future learning physical environments; it is proving to be an effective design tool because it enhances users' capacity to have an effective impact on the work environment. The process simulation method can be illustrated with the aid of the figure below.

The different phases of the process simulation method

In addition to a phenomenological analysis, which is useful when dealing with verbal answers and pictorial responses, a hermeneutic approach was used to broaden the concepts and find points of convergence. Our study was based on the notion that by describing school authorities' and users' different perceptions; we could reach an accurate overall impression of a high-quality physical learning environment. One element of the study involved evaluating the quality of the latter: this was understood to be a value judgement resulting from users' everyday experiences and their subsequent interpretation of them (Heidegger, 2000; Marton and Booth, 1997).

Study Findings

The results of the study highlighted several key factors relating to a quality physical learning environment, namely the relevance for school users of the teaching space as a whole as well as their specific needs in relation to furniture and equipment. It showed that the physical learning environment is pivotal to users' desire to develop the school's operational environment as well as their need to renew its operational culture. The more meaningful and challenging the operational environment is, the more the user is willing to improve the physical learning environment. The needs of teachers, head-teachers and students call for practical solutions, and these too have an impact on it.

When physical learning environments offer resources and possibilities that support new teaching methods and learning goals, schools are much more prompt to change their operational culture. In other words, they are important when developing school operational culture, as well as work environments. Despite the differences within education systems, the basic principles of using physical learning environments and the concepts behind ideal teaching spaces are very similar. The study's findings indicate that pressure for change in teaching and learning is felt at the national level. Consequently, the expectations for physical learning environments do not differ significantly between countries. Moreover, today's well-educated and committed teachers offer a largely unharnessed resource for planning and implementing future learning environments.

Once the designs by participating students had been examined, a single model was selected. A mock-up of it was made and tested by groups of students. The resulting simulation provided a prime example of a learning space that supports teaching and learning operations, while demonstrating flexibility, sustainability and modifiability. The model is illustrated below.

The ideal learning space

Future technological advances and developments in social networks and media, as well as different teaching and learning methods, will undoubtedly require dynamic teaching spaces. The design of the proposed model takes these factors into account: the carefully conceived flexible layout and furniture arrangement facilitates individual, pair and group work methods. The simultaneous enhanced interaction between the student and the teacher, on the one hand, and the physical environment, on the other, optimizes new information flows (Lehtinen, 1997).Respondents perceived the traditional classroom as a passive area, which hindered the full use of space.

They associated dynamic teaching spaces with flexibility and the possibility of creating different furniture configurations. The latter can be achieved by ensuring that furniture is mobile and that there is free and easy access to information technology. A dynamic teaching space concept is summarized below

A dynamic teaching space concept

The study participants did not decry the traditional classroom as such, but they called for additional spaces of different sizes in optimal locations to support teaching and learning processes. The spaces should offer various possibilities for learning to take place: this can range from individual study to large group activities.

They should also support teacher coaching and individual work. Such flexibility fosters new types of teaching and learning, as illustrated above, which are determined by the demands of the subject or activity. In order to be successful, the sustainable physical learning environment needs to be equipped with both modular workstations and areas with comfortable seating, which contribute to support individual learning. It should be possible to adapt the furniture to different configurations.

Similarly, as teaching and information technology tools facilitate flexible teaching, it should be easy to displace equipment and wireless terminals according to different subjects and work methods.

Conclusion

Nuikkinen (2009, p. 278) argues that users' expectations and the theoretical concept of what makes a good school building do not match up. In practice, this runs counter – to a certain extent – to traditional planning, which on the whole requires teachers and students, as users of the buildings, to adapt to given environments (Dudek, 2000; Sanoff, 2009).

The research findings were clear: all participants recognized that significant changes must be implemented to the physical learning environment to better support users' needs. Pedagogical and physical structures need to be remodeled in parallel so as to respond to the challenges posed by changes in schools' operational culture. In order for a school to develop into a dynamic physical learning environment, there needs to be a behavioural change in relation to planning and producing spatial solutions. Change cannot occur without input from teachers and students – the main school users. Teachers and students who conceived the study applauded the significant shift away from the traditional classroom and said how much they would like to work in a similar space. If a school provides a quality environment for students, this will facilitate the acquisition of skills that are important for society. The choice of equipment is important: it should be versatile, resistant, durable and easy to repair. User-based innovative processes should be at the heart of designing the physical learning environment of tomorrow's schools. This process should take into account the global needs of students, teachers, school administrators and the community, while respecting the environment. A judicious selection of products and services that minimizes negative environmental impacts will also be of benefit to all.

References

1. Dudek, M. (2000), Architecture of Schools: The New Learning Environments, Architectural Press, Oxford, p. xiv.
2. Evagorou, M. et al. (2009), "An Investigation of the Potential of Interactive Simulations for Developing System Thinking Skills in Elementary School: A Case Study with Fifth-Graders and Sixth-Graders", International Journal of Science Education, Vol. 31, Issue 5, pp. 356.
3. Heidegger, M. (2000), Oleminen ja aika, translated into Finnish by R. Kupiainen, Vastapaino, Tampere, pp. 33-34, 80, 84.
4. Heitor, T. (2005), "Potential problems and challenges in defining international design principles for school", Evaluating Quality in Educational Facilities, pp. 48, OECD/PEB, www.oecd.org/edu/facilities/evaluatingquality. Lehtinen, E. (1997), Verkkopedagogiikka, Edita, Helsinki.
5. Marton, F. and S. Booth (1997), Learning and Awareness, Lawrence Erlbaum Associates, Mahwah, New Jersey, p. 13.

6. Mononen-Aaltonen, M. (1998), "A Learning Environment – A Euphemism for Instruction or a Potential for Dialogue?", Media Education Publication 8, pp. 163–212.

7. OECD (Organisation for Economic Co-operation and Development) (2006), CELE Organising Framework on Evaluating Quality in Educational Spaces, www.oecd.org/edu/facilities/evaluatingquality.

8. OECD (2009), International Pilot Study on the Evaluation of Quality In Educational Spaces (EQES), User Manual, www.oecd.org/edu/facilities/evaluatingquality.

9. Sanoff, H. (2009), Research Based Design of an Elementary School, Open House International, Vol. 34, No. 1, pp. 9-16.

10. Smeds, R. et al. (2006), "SimLab Process Simulation Method as a Boundary Object for Inter-organizational Innovation", Multidisciplinary Research on Simulation Methods and Educational Games in Industrial Management, proceedings of the 10th International Workshop on Experimental Interactive Learning in Industrial Management, Trondheim, Norway, June.

11. Smeds, R. et al. (2007), "Process Simulation for Social Innovation Case: Planning the School for the Future", Multidisciplinary Research on New Methods for Learning and Innovation in Enterprise Networks, proceedings of the 11th Special Interest Group Workshop on Experimental Learning in Industrial Management, 20-22 May, Bremen, Germany, pp. 177–191.

14

Flipping Class Rooms-a Boon to Quality Education

Introduction

Bloom's taxonomy has been considered as a cornerstone of learning and it was revised as recently as 2000 (Bloom, 1956; Pohl, 2000). Bloom's taxonomy divides learning objectives into three domains: Cognitive, affective and psychomotor (Krathwohl, Bloom, & Masia, 1973; Pohl, 2000; Simpson, 1972). According to Bloom (1984), an average student who receives one-on-one attention is enabled by constant feedback and corrective process, and can jump into the 98th percentile of the student population in academic achievement. Although his study caught educators' attention, it hasn't changed the standard teaching practices, mostly because one-on-one instruction is too expensive (Thompson, 2011).

New approaches in using technologies, however, have started to present great potentials for incorporating sound pedagogies into classroom teaching without incurring additional cost. The purpose of this paper is to describe called "flipped homework versus classroom equation" by some (e.g. Kahn, 2011), and "inverted teaching/ classroom" by others (e.g., Lage, Platt, & Treglia, 2000)

What is a 'flipped classroom'?

The flipped classroom describes a **reversal of traditional teaching** where students gain first exposure to new material outside of class, usually via reading or lecture videos, and then class time is used to do the harder work of assimilating that knowledge through strategies such as problem-solving, discussion or debates. The purpose of flipping the classroom is to shift from **passive** to **active learning** to focus on the higher order thinking skills such as analysis, synthesis and evaluation (Bloom). There are many permutations of what a flipped classroom will look like and depends on variables such as class size, resources, support and readiness to change.

The flipped class room is

1. a means to increase interaction and personalized contact between students and teachers;
2. an environment where students take responsibility for their own learning;
3. a class-room where the teacher is not the "sage on the stage", but the "guide on the side";
4. a blending of direct instruction with constructive learning;
5. a class where all students are engaged in learning;
6. a place where students take more responsibility for their own learning and get personalized education.

Why Flip?

The main goal in flipping a class is to cultivate deeper, richer, active learning experiences for students when the instructor is present to coach and guide them. Emphasis is on higher-order thinking skills and application to complex problems and may include collaborative learning, individual based learning, peer instructions and problem sets.

Flipped Classroom

A new method of teaching is turning the traditional classroom on its head. Flip teaching or a flipped classroom is a form of blended learning in which students learn new content online by watching video lectures, usually at home, and what used to be homework is now done in class with teachers offering more personalized guidance and interaction with students, instead of lecturing. This is also known as backwards classroom, flipped classroom, reverse teaching, and the Thayer Method.

Traditional vs. flipped teaching

The traditional pattern of teaching has been to assign students to read textbooks and work on problem sets outside school, while listening to lectures and taking tests in class. In flip teaching, the students first study the topic by themselves, typically using video lessons prepared by the teacher or third parties. In class, students apply the knowledge by solving problems and doing practical work. The teacher tutors the students when they become stuck, rather than imparting the initial lesson in person. Complementary techniques include differentiated instruction and project-based learning. Flipped classrooms free class time for hands-on work. Students learn by doing and asking questions.

History

Eric Mazur developed peer instruction in the 1990s. He found that computer-aided instruction allowed him to coach instead of lecture. In 2004, Salman Khan began to record videos at the request of a younger cousin who felt that recorded lessons would let her skip parts she had mastered and replay parts that were troubling her. Khan's model essentially provides one-to-one tutoring. Khan Academy videos are used as part of some educators' flipped teaching strategy.

Flipped mastery

Traditionally, each topic in class receives a fixed amount of time for all students. Students who do not master the material get no extra time. Mastery learning is stressed, by requiring each student to master the topic before moving to the next one. *Flipped mastery learning* applies the mastery concept to flipped classrooms. Mastery learning was briefly popular in the 1920s, and was revived by Benjamin Bloom in 1968. It has shown dramatic success. The teacher provides materials, tools and support. Students set goals and manage their time. In a flipped mastery classroom, students view each lecture and work on each exercise or project when they have mastered the precursors.

The key elements of the flipped classroom:

1. Provides an opportunity for students to gain first exposure prior to class. The mechanism used for first exposure can vary, from simple textbook readings to lecture videos to podcasts or screen casts.
2. Provides an incentive for students to prepare for class. The assignment can vary from online quizzes to worksheets to short writing assignments, but in each case the task provides an incentive for students to come to class prepared.
3. Provides a mechanism to assess student understanding. The pre-class assignments that students complete as evidence of their preparation can also help both the instructor and the student assess understanding.

Educational Implications of Flipped Class-rooms

1. Provides competence to students to have a deeper foundation of factual knowledge and understand facts and ideas in the context of conceptual frame work.
2. Provides an opportunity for the students to use their factual knowledge while they have access to immediate feedback from peers and instructor.
3. Helps students to correct their misconceptions and organize their new knowledge for future use.
4. Through a meta-cognitive approach helps students learn to take control of their own learning by defining learning goals and mentoring their progress in achieving them.

References

1. Anderson LW and Krathwohl D (2001). *A taxonomy for learning, teaching, and assessing: a revision of Bloom's taxonomy of educational objectives.* New York: Longman.

2. Berrett D (2012). How 'flipping' the classroom can improve the traditional lecture. *The Chronicle of Higher Education*, Feb. 19, 2012.
3. http://www.cirtl.net/node/7788 and http://derekbruff.org/?p=901.
4. http://en.wikipedia.org/wiki/Flip_teachin
5. https://ctl.utexas.edu/teaching/flipping_a_class/what_is_flipped
6. http://www.flippedclassroom.com/

15

Innovative Technologies in Teacher Education

Introduction

Educational Technology has great potential for improving the teaching-learning process. Educational technology is the development, application and evaluation of systems, techniques and also aids in the field of human learning. One of the important contributions of educational technology is individualized instruction, which enable s us to make use of self-instructional programmes.
Teacher-centered and group-centered approaches are inadequate since they hardly make any provision for individual differences of the learners. The premise is that, strictly speaking, no two students in the class are alike and that there are many permuations and combinations of individual differences.

Need for Individualized Instruction

We have three categories of learners in our classrooms, viz., Brilliant/Gifted, Average, below average/ Slow learners. Frankly speaking, the teachers can satisfy the first two categories of the learners in the class rooms. We must give individual attention to the slow learners and transform them into average learners. Individualized instruction is not only the best option for slow learners but it can also be used to the other two categories of learners.

Individualized instruction means, learners are learning at their own pace. The learner is not forced to move with the other learners of the class. Such an approach creates confidence in him. There are many methods in individualized instruction, viz., Assignment, Learner Controlled Instruction, Programmed Instruction, Personalized System of Instruction, Computer Assisted Instruction, etc. The recent method of individualized instruction in the field of education is 'e-Learning'.

E-Learning

E-Learning is the online delivery of information, communication, education and training, which has been defined to increase learner's knowledge and skills so that they can be more productive. E-Learning has different types of learning technologies viz., web-based learning, interactive distance learning, internet-based learning, CD-ROM etc. The advantages of e-Learning are online demand, availability, self-pacing, interactivity and confidence, etc.

E-Content

E-Content means web-based instruction developed for individuals' auto learning on any subject required by the learners. The benefits of e-Content for learners are including flexible schedule and instruction at convenient locations-homes, schools and colleges. It informs learners about their progress and accomplishment. An important outcome of e-Learning is e-Content. E-Learning is a process and e-content is a product. Many private institutions have come forward to prepare e-content materials for a limited number of subjects. At the higher education level, the University Grants Commission, New Delhi has allocated funds to those who are willing to develop 'e-Content' on any subject. A few colleges have already started 'e-Content development cell'. All the school level, it is in the infancy stage. According to Information Technology Policy, the

Directorate of School Education, Government of Tamil Nadu has planned to introduce web-based instruction in the schools from 2010-2011 onwards.

E-Content Package

E-Content package can be used as teacher in the classroom situation. While we are developing an e-Content package, we must know and link it with ADDIE model. There are more than 100 different instructional design models, but almost all are based on the generic "ADDIE model". The ADDIE model is a systematic instructional design model, which was redefined by Dick and Carey and others in 1996. The five phases of ADDIE model has five steps. Each step has an outcome that feeds the subsequent step as follows:

1. Analysis Phase
2. Design Phase
3. Development Phase
4. Implementation Phase
5. Evaluation Phase

Development of E-Content Package

The following steps are to be involved in developing an e-Content package on the basis of ADDIE model.

I. Analysis Phase

In the analysis phase the following steps are to be followed:

1. Selection of system / stage

In school education, we have different education systems viz. Tamil Nadu State Board (TNSB), Central Board of Secondary Education (CBSE) and Indian School Certificate (ISC). We can decide on any one of the systems.

In higher education, we have different disciplines. We can select any one of the disciplines to develop an e-Content programme with the help of faculties in different disciplines.

2. Selection of target group

We have to select a target group: the school college university learners. General information of the learners can be collected viz., Name, Sex, Group studying, Name of the institution, Locality of the institution, Kind of the institution, Study habit, Computer courses undergone, Internet facility, and Browsing habit.

3. Selection of the unit

The development of e-Content can be applied to all the subjects. Selection of the unit will be decided after thorough discussion with the subject experts and faculties / teachers of the concerned subjects on the basis of the following points:

(i) Whether the lecture method is sufficient to deliver the instruction to the students.

(ii) Whether the media option is to be used to deliver the instruction.

(iii) Whether animations or graphics are to be utilized in the instruction.

4. Decision on duration of the programme

After consulting with the subject experts and faculties teachers of the concerned subjects, duration of the e-Content programmed will be finalized. Allotment of duration / sessions will be fixed on the basis of the curricula of the subjects.

5. Developing the instructional objectives of the programme

The instructional objectives can be decided on the basis of the behavioral changes to be expected from the learners after going through the e-Content programme developed.

6. Classification of Students

A pre-requisite test consisting of basic units of the subject, can be conducted for classifying three categories of learners, viz., Brilliant, Average and Slow learners.

II. Design Phase

1. Consultation with the subject experts and faculties / teachers

Script for e-Content can be planned in consultation with the subject experts and faculties / teachers of the concerned subjects in which the following things are discussed.

(i) What are the aspects to be covered?

(ii) Where are audio and video clippings to be added in the programme?

2. Consultation with the media experts and software programmers.

E-Script for e-Content is planned in consultation with the media experts and software programmers to decide where graphics and animation to be added in the instruction and how audio and video clipping are to be added in the e-script.

III. Development Phase

1. Preparation of the script

Contents of the script for the programme are prepared on the basis of discussion with the discussion with the subject experts and faculties / teachers of the concerned subjects. The contents are to be organized logically as well as psychologically and an ideal balance is to be struck on the basis of relevant literature, text books, work-books, manuals and other reference material.

2. Preparation of e-script

After preparation of the content script, it is to be converted into e-Script on the basis of consultation with software programmers and media experts. E-Script is considered in the following aspects:

(i) Audio and video clippings

(ii) Linkages between one content to another content

(iii) Graphics and Animation

(iv) Exercises of the programme to be done by the students.

(v) Explanations to the concepts

3. Editing the e-Script

After the first draft, the e-script is to be edited at the following three levels.

(i) Technical accuracy editing is to be done for ensuring technical accuracy of the subject in consultation with subject experts

(ii) Programme technique editing is to be done for aptness of the illustrations used in the script.

(iii) Composition editing is to be done for correcting grammatical errors, checking spelling, punctuations and sequence of information etc.

4. Developing the instructional objectives of the programme

The instructional objectives can be decided on the basis of the behavioral changes to be expected from the learners after going through the e-Content programme developed.

Conclusion

(i) A cell for e-Content should be established in all the schools, colleges and universities. Faculties of the schools, colleges and universities should be involved to prepare e-Content packages in their respective subjects.

(ii) University's Education Departments, Educational Multi-media Research Centers and Colleges of Education should train the faculties of the schools, colleges and universities for preparation of e-Content.

(iii) Useful subject oriented web sites can be created and also utilized to deliver the validated e-Content packages for the benefit of the learners.

(iv) Continuous Assessment cell on e-Content will be established for improvement of the programme.

References

1. Aggarwal, J.C., (1999) Essentials of Educational Technology: Teaching learning Innovations in Education, New Delhi, Vikas Publishing House Pvt. Ltd.

2. Dick, W., & Carey, L. (1996) the Systematic Design of Instruction (4th Edn.) New York: Harper Collins College Publishers.

3. Leshin. C.B., Pollock, J., & Reigeluth, C.M. (1992) Instructional Design Strategies and Tactics. Englewood Cliffs, NJ: Educational Technology Publication.

16

Flipped Classroom

Introduction

At present, the flipped class becomes more popular, new tools may emerge to support the out-of-class portion of the curriculum. Greater number of tools, they support to the active and collaborative work common in the elements of the flipped classroom, supplementing traditional out-of-class work with video presentations and supporting project-based and lab-style efforts. The flipped classroom model is revolutionizing teaching methods and strategies around the globe, addressing these concerns by creating time for individualized 1:1 instruction between teachers and students. Flipped classrooms are a reversed teaching model that "flips" the settings for instruction and homework.

In a flipped class, instruction is provided to students at home through video or Internet based lectures and class time is used to complete homework-like assignments. By moving instruction to the home and homework to the class, students are given more 1:1 time with their teacher to work through their assignments. This 1:1 time helps to ensure that each student fully understands the key concepts presented in each lesson plan before moving on to the next lesson.

Does it improve Learning?

Yes, the flipped classrooms are improving education around the world is because the role of the teacher has been flipped from a lecturer to a tutor. The focus of the classroom transforms one-size fits all instruction into individualized coaching.

Flexibility in class room

The notion of a flipped classroom draws on such concepts as active learning, student engagement, hybrid course design, and course pod casting. The value of a flipped class is in the repurposing of class time into a workshop where students can inquire about lecture content, test their skills in applying knowledge, and interact with one another in hands-on activities. During class sessions, instructors function as coaches or advisors, encouraging students in individual inquiry and collaborative effort.

It means

"flipping the classroom" means that students gain first exposure to new material outside of class, usually via reading or lecture videos, and then use class time to do the harder work of assimilating that knowledge, perhaps through problem-solving, discussion, or debates. The flipped classroom is a pedagogical model in which the typical lecture and homework elements of a course are reversed. Short video lectures are viewed by students at home before the class session, while in-class time is devoted to exercises, projects, or discussions. The video lecture is often seen as the key ingredient in the flipped approach, such lectures being either created by the instructor and posted online or selected from an online repository.

Bloom's Taxonomy (Revised)

In terms of Bloom's revised taxonomy (2001), this means that students are doing the lower levels of cognitive work (gaining knowledge and comprehension) outside of class, and focusing on the higher forms of cognitive work (application, analysis, synthesis, and/or evaluation) in class, where they have the support of their peers and instructor. This model contrasts from the traditional model in which "first exposure" occurs via lecture in class, with students assimilating knowledge through homework; thus the term "flipped classroom."

Traditional classroom

1. Which is teacher focused.
2. Content is introduced during the class time.
3. Students apply at home only.

Flipped class room

1. Student focused.
2. Content is introduced at home.
3. Students apply at school.
4. Teacher to assist as needed.

Difference

S.No	Traditional classroom	Flipped classroom
1.	Teacher centered	Student centered.
2.	Teacher lecturing in school, Book work at home.	Lecturing at home and Book work in school.
3.	Teacher stands at the board. Spending more time for lecturing.	Teacher interacts more with students. More time for lab work. Students can be more effective.
4.	Students passively watch the demonstration.	Students are actively involved in the demonstration.
5.	Parents do not know what is going on in school.	Parents watch the class at home.

The key elements of the flipped classroom

1. Provide an opportunity for students to gain first exposure prior to class.
2. Provide an incentive for students to prepare for class.
3. Provide a mechanism to assess student understanding.
4. Provide in-class activities that focus on higher level cognitive activities.

When?

We use Flip classroom instruction when the content is challenging. Topics that the students will struggle on are great topics to flip. When we flip our instruction the students need greater differentiation, support, review, remediation, and engagement. It is the perfect time for to know students will benefit from plenty of face to face interaction and when we have a highly interactive involved activity. Students get to apply, discuss, and make connections with the topic.

Flipped instruction is for topics that need greater depth of understanding. It is not for memorizing procedures. It is a technique that meets the demands of the Common Core in developing the complex problem solving abilities of students.

How?

A model in which students gain ***first-exposure learning*** prior to class and focus on the *processing* part of learning (synthesizing, analyzing, problem-solving, etc.) in class. To ensure that students do the preparation necessary for productive class time, in this assignment-based model in which students produce work (writing, problems, etc.) prior to class. The students receive productive feedback through the processing activities that occur during class, reducing the need for the instructor to provide extensive written feedback on the students' work. Now traditional lecture format is incompatible, with some learning styles to make their course more compatible with their students' varied learning styles; we should designed an inverted classroom in which we provided students with a variety of tools to gain first exposure to material outside of class: textbook readings, lecture videos, PowerPoint presentations with voice-over, and printable PowerPoint slides.

There is no single model for the flipped classroom—the term is widely used to describe almost any class structure that provides pre-recorded lectures followed by in-class exercises. In one common model, students might view multiple lectures of five to seven minutes each. Online quizzes or activities can be to test what students have learned. Immediate quiz feedback and the ability to rerun lecture segments may help clarify points of confusion. Instructors might lead in-class discussions or turn the classroom into a studio where students create, collaborate, and put into practice what they learned from the lectures they view outside class. Because Flipped class room approach represents a comprehensive change in the class dynamic.

Why?

In a traditional lecture, students often try to capture what is being said at the instant the speaker says it. They cannot stop to reflect upon what is being said, and they may miss significant points because they are trying to transcribe the instructor's words. By contrast, the use of video and other prerecorded media puts lectures under the control of the students: they can watch, rewind, and fast-forward as needed. This ability may be of particular value to students with accessibility concerns, especially where captions are provided for those with hearing impairments. Devoting class time to application of concepts might give instructors a better opportunity to detect errors in thinking, particularly those that are widespread in a class. At the same time, collaborative projects can encourage social interaction among students, making it easier for them to learn from one another and for those of varying skill levels to support their peers.

It allows for greater differentiation in meeting student needs. Students are able to review and replay the instructional segment as many times as necessary. A variety of strategies and materials can be provided to meet the various student needs. This provides for those students who wish to move through the material quickly. While those who need to take their time and process are also able to. Students have greater control over their learning.

By flipping classroom instruction, the teacher is able to offer greater support. The teacher is present while students struggle with the application of the knowledge. The teacher is there to respond to needs and answer questions. It is possible to give small group assistance and work one-on-one with the students that need help.

Using the flipped instructional model, teachers and students can spend more time working together and delving into complex problems. Teachers are better able to meet Common Core Standards. Students who need extra review and remediation have the instruction at their fingertips. They can review and study the instruction as often as necessary. Materials are archived and ready as needed.

Implications

The flipped classroom constitutes a role change for instructors, who give up their front-of-the-class position in favor of a more collaborative and co-operative contribution to the teaching process. There is a concomitant change in the role of students, many of whom are used to being cast as passive participants in the education process, where instruction is served to them. The flipped model puts more of the responsibility for learning on the shoulders of students while giving them greater impetus to experiment. Activities can be student-led, and communication among students can become the determining dynamic of a session devoted to learning through hands-on work. What the flip does particularly well is to bring about a distinctive shift in priorities— from merely covering material to working toward mastery of it.

Benefits

1. Students learn at varying speed.
2. Students are provided opportunities for review lessons front-load for classroom activities.
3. Materials are ready and prepared for students who are absent or sick.
4. Parents can view lessons and better assists students.
5. Students do not struggle with completing homework because they forgot how it does.
6. Students are actively working with their peers.
7. Students take ownership of their learning.
8. Personalized educations for slow and fast learners.
9. Greater opportunity for 1:1 help from teachers.
10. Stronger bonds with teachers.

11. Encouragement to collaborate on ideas and projects with other students.
12. Ability to rewind, save, review lesson plans at any moment.

Conclusion

"To develop competence in an area of inquiry, students must: a) have a deep foundation of factual knowledge, b) understand facts and ideas in the context of a conceptual framework, and c) organize knowledge in ways that facilitate retrieval and application" By providing an opportunity for students to *use* their new factual knowledge while they have access to immediate feedback from peers and the instructor, The flipped classroom helps students learn to correct misconceptions and organize their new knowledge such that it is more accessible for future use. Furthermore, the immediate feedback that occurs in the flipped classroom also helps students recognize and think about their own growing understanding,

The classroom an effective flip requires careful preparation. Recording lectures requires effort and time on the part of faculty, and out-of-class and in-class elements must be carefully integrated for students to understand the model and be motivated to prepare for class. As a result, introducing a flip can mean additional work and may require new skills for the instructor, although this learning curve could be mitigated by entering the model slowly. Students, for their part, have been known to complain about the loss of face-to-face lectures, particularly if they feel the assigned video lectures are available to anyone online. Students with this perspective may not immediately appreciate the value of the hands-on portion of the model, wondering what their tuition brings them. Finally, even where students embrace the model, their equipment and access might not always support rapid delivery of video. During the hands-on activities students got better grasp of the information and more confidence in what he has learned than he could have gotten from an in-class lecture.

References

1. Berrett D (2012). How 'flipping' the classroom can improve the traditional lecture. *The Chronicle of Higher Education*, Feb. 19, 2012.

2. Anderson LW and Krathwohl D (2001). *A taxonomy for learning, teaching, and assessing: a revision of Bloom's taxonomy of educational objectives.* New York: Longman.
3. Bransford JD, Brown AL, and Cocking RR (2000). *How people learn: Brain, mind, experience, and school.* Washington, D.C.: National Academy Press.
4. Crouch CH and Mazur E (2001). Peer instruction: Ten years of experience and results. *American Journal of Physics* 69: 970-977.
5. DesLauriers L, Schelew E, and Wieman C (2011). Improved learning in a large-enrollment physics class. *Science* 332: 862-864.
6. Fitzpatrick M (2012). Classroom lectures go digital. *The New York Times,* June 24, 2012.
7. Hake R (1998). Interactive-engagement versus traditional methods: A six-thousand-student survey of mechanics test data for introductory physics courses. *American Journal of Physics* 66: 64-74.
8. Lage MJ, Platt GJ, and Treglia M (2000). Inverting the classroom: A gateway to creating an inclusive learning environment. *The Journal of Economic Education* 31: 30-43.
9. Novak G, Patterson ET, Gavrin AD, and Christian W (1999). *Just-in-Time Teaching: Blending Active Learning with Web Technology.* Upper Saddle River, NJ: Prentice Hall.
10. Pashler H, McDaniel M, Rohrer D, and Bjork R (2008). Learning styles: Concepts and evidence. Psychological Science in the Public Interest 9: 103-119.
11. Walvoord BE, and Anderson VJ (1998). *Effective grading: A tool for learning and assessment.* San Francisco: Jossey-Bass.

17

Flipped classroom for B.Ed., students

A flipped classroom is one form of blended learning. The blended delivery model adopted in this case study uses online content delivery mechanisms for both curriculum and evaluation. This approach allows students to better utilize face-to-face class time to have in-depth discussions with teaching staff on application of knowledge. This cast study describes the experience of both students and staff in relation to this major redesign as well as provides some reflective commentary in relation to the pilot. The pilot described in this paper relates to a B.Ed., Students. This paper will describe the process of unit redesign and implementation, including planning tools developed for teaching staff and students. The case study also reveals that student readiness and self-management skills perhaps are one of the most important elements that result in a successful student blended learning experience.

In 2007, Jonathan Bergam and Aaron Sams, Who were teaching at a high school in Colorado, recognized that student absences led to students who were missing key concepts presented in class. In order to deliver these students the material, Bergman and Sams created videos of class lectures. The videos were subsequently made available to other students in class who wanted to re-watch lectures and review the material. This sparked an idea; why not have all students watch the videos at home and use class time to reinforce the material that has been learned.

The flipped model takes the traditional model of teaching; presenting information in a lecture format during class, while reinforcing the information at home through worksheets, and flips the location at where these occur. Under the flipped model, students watch lecture videos at home and get an opportunity to enhance their learning in the classroom with other students.

The University of Western Sydney in 2012 launched a three year learning and teaching enhancement project. The project aims to fuel the growth in the use of appropriate information and communication technologies (ICTs) in the delivery of learning and teaching to meet the needs of an ever increasing technological dependent student population. This project objective is to improve the student's learning experience and implement curriculum change, introduce flexibility in study regimes and overall incorporate innovation resulting in educational excellence.

A review of the literature would suggest that, blended learning is a loosely defined term by scholars, which essentially refers to the integration of both classroom and online delivery methods (Partridge, Ponting and McCay, 2011). In the unit chosen for this pilot made use of a flipped classroom, for both delivery of content and assessment. In a 'flipped' classroom, students acquire content knowledge online by watching mini-lecture series and completing learning activities, and then come to face-to-face sessions to apply what they have learned in class (Bergmann and Sams, 2012). The pilot sought to evaluate whether a flipped classroom teaching strategy would achieve desired learning outcomes teaching models in a better way, which focus on both in a better way than the traditional teaching models used in this unit to date. It was thought that a blended approach might improve both knowledge acquisition and application of the curriculum. The blended learning model also seeks to provide students more control and flexibility over their learning and, at the same time, respond to the growing pressures resulting from increasing student enrolments and class sizes.

Design

The pilot B.Ed, all the subject of unit previously adopted a didactic teaching method, which was offered in the traditional lecture-tutorial mode. All teaching activities were done face-to-face. In the new design, the content topics covered remain very similar to the previous taught curriculum however delivery was drastically different. The changes have been summarized in Table 1.

Table 1: Curriculum changes in the selected first year management accounting unit

	Previous version (traditional teaching method)	New version (flipped classroom teaching method)
Teaching activities	Two hour face-to-face lecture Two hour face-to-face tutorial	One-hour equivalent online learning module One hour face to face demonstration workshop Two hour face-to-face tutorial
Assessments	10% Teaching Competency 10% Internal Assessments 25% Record based 55% Final exam (paper-based)	10% Online Teaching Competency (students are required to achieve a minimum score of 70% in 8/10 sessions) 15% Internal Assessments (paper-based; handed out and marked in tutorials) 25% Records based (online Submission; administered in computer lab) 50% Final exam (paper-based)
Feedback	In class; paper-based	Instant and personalized online feedback; in class; paper-based

To design a one-hour equivalent online learning module for each teaching session, a topic planner was used as a tool. The topic planner helped the lecturer to break a traditional lecture into several discrete modules with a variety of learning activities within each. These activities included recorded lecture content videos, external learning resources, real life case studies, knowledge quizzes as well as reflective activities. The planner also required the lecturer to give estimations on how much time students were expected to spend on each task, which helped the lecturer to design and review online modules from a student's perspective.

All lecture content videos were recorded by using Echo 360 personal capture, including both screen and webcam captures. The lengths of videos were varied from 3 minutes to 10 minutes. Full learning modules were delivered via Blackboard, the Learning Management System centrally supported by the University. Extra features were enabled, including Teachers Personality feature for each learning module, which was set as a self-checking point for students to record their learning progresses.

Online homework and Record were delivered on an external platform called 'My Accounting Lab'. The platform is designed to facilitate learning and teaching activities in accounting education. My Accounting Lab offers Teaching Competency, Internal Assessments, Record based, final exam (paper-based) and instant feedback. In this unit, students could access My Accounting Lab by following instructions post on the Blackboard site.

Table 2: Weekly learning planner for students

	Task	**Description**	**Form**	**Recommended time on task**
1	Reading	Weekly reading of selected chapters	Offline	45 - 60 min
2	Online activities	A variety of online activities which are designed to assist students in developing a further understanding of the topic	Online (Blackboard)	60 min
3	Demonstration Workshop	In-depth discussions & problem solving demonstration	Face-to-face	60 min
4	Online learning activities	Pre-selected questions from My Accounting Lab with feedback	Online (Blackboard)	120 -180 min
5	Tutorial	Further feedback from the tutor Unseen problems	Face-to-face	120 min
		Recommended time on designed learning tasks for each week:		8 hours
		Students are also required to spend another 2 hours per week on individual learning tasks, such as, reviewing and exam preparation.		

In order to effectively communicate with students and help students to orientate in a blended unit, a weekly learning planner was designed. The planner contained information on what tasks students were expected to complete, recommended learning order and time on task for each week. The information is shown in Table 2.

Implementation

The newly designed unit was offered TNTEU, 2013-14, which was from August to June. Prior to the beginning of the year of moth, training was conducted for the teaching team. The Blackboard unit site was constructed and releases to students prior to the beginning of semester .This release include detailed instructions in relation to the online delivery approach as well as the first two learning modules. A welcome email was sent to all students introducing the new teaching approach and informed them that more support information could be found in the 'Getting started' session on Blackboard.

In week of begging, the Blackboard site was visited by more than fifty percent of enrolled students. More than twenty percent of enrolled students claimed, by toggling the 'marked review' feature, that they have completed the first learning module before the class started.

In the first tutorial class, online activities were demonstrated to students and the weekly learning planner was explicitly explained. Students were also encouraged to share their understandings on how to learn the unit with their classmates.

Another weeks into the year, the teaching team reported a highly positive experience that students were well prepared before they came to tutorial classes. Blackboard tracking data, which showed that over eighty percent of students were actively using the learning modules, also supported the observation made by the teaching team. In the first four weeks, the content areas of the unit site attracted students.

However, the growing momentum seemed to fade after week four. Despite the fact that the teaching team regularly communicated with students both in face-to-face sessions and in the blackboard site via Announcements, student activity in Blackboard started to decline. After a sharp drop after the Record based, it gradually climbed back before the final exam.

The online midyear invigilated on campus and students received marks and feedback immediately upon submission. The overall student performance was acceptable but lower than the expectation from the teaching team. The team, then, quickly adjusted certain teaching strategies, in particular, the design of homework. The total number of questions for each week was reduced; however, more procedure questions were added. As a result, the paper based final exam indicated a positive performance shift in the cohort from pass grade to credit and distinctions.

Student experience and discussion

The teaching team has been collecting feedback from students during the year. After the census day, there were 100 students who were officially enrolled in the unit. Most of students were keen to express their opinions of blended learning. They provided both verbal and written feedback on their learning experience.

Student experience has been summarized as below:

1. The majority of students reported that this unit was their first blended learning experience.
2. Students who have followed the learning planner tended to report positive learning experience while students
3. The majority of students claimed that they have received sufficient instructions and feedback.
4. Most of students claimed that they have spent less than one-hour study time on completing online learning modules, which was less than the estimation from the teaching team
5. Positive feedback from students appreciated the richness of learning resources, learning flexibility and practical online homework with instant feedback.
6. Negative feedback from students did not like the unit design because it required students to complete too many tasks, which were time-consuming.

Future Changes as a Result of Feedback

1. Review the curriculum design of online learning modules and demonstration workshops.

(To optimize content knowledge delivery to meet the needs of different learning styles)

2. Review the design and assessment weightings of My Accounting Lab.

   (To make a better use of computer-based online activities)

3. Provide 'just-in-time' instructions to students during the year.

   (To improve the clarity of instructions and provide better scaffolds to students)

Implications

The flipped classroom experience in B.Ed., students has implications for blended learning development in accounting education. It explores more flexible and interactive ways to use ICTs to deliver a unit that is traditionally seen as a hands-on, technical and boring unit. Despite mixed responses from students, the teaching team is enthused by the facts that students were truly engaged in the first four weeks and the results of final exam demonstrated an encouraging student performance shift. More work will be done to investigate how to sustain student engagement in blended learning. The emerging issues on assessing and addressing student readiness for blended learning require further research.

References

1. Bergmann, J. & Sams, A. (2012). Flip Your Classroom: Reach Every Student in Every Class Every Day. International Society for Technology in Education.30th ascilite Conference 2013 Proceedings Page 255

2. Partridge, H., Ponting, D., & McCay, M., (2011). Good practice report: blended Learning. Australian Learning and Teaching Council. http://eprints.qut.edu.au/47566.

18

E-learning: Knowledge Packaging – Quality Enhancement in Education

Introduction

Information revolution and knowledge society are the two most important buzzwords of the 21st century. A revolution is taking place in education with the introduction of computers in education. The rapid evolution of Information and Communication Technologies (ICTS) and the emergence of the information society create numerous new opportunities for the improvement of the quality of education. Personalized Learning (PL) is widely considered as one promising direction towards the full exploitation of the potential for the information society in education. Personalized learning advocates that it is the learning context that should be adapted to the individual learner, as opposed to "traditional" learning settings, where it is the learner's responsibility to adapt to the learning context in order to maximize the "learning outcome".

Modern information technologies are transforming the way people learn. E-learning provides new possibilities for personalized learning at home or in the workplace, reduces the need for costly classroom training and enables an optimal balance between traditional and innovative forms of knowledge transfer.

A knowledge worker can do the following knowledge activities such as -

1. Knowledge creation
2. Knowledge packaging
3. Knowledge distribution
4. Knowledge application

Teachers and institution around the world are creating and sharing learning materials and courses for use on e-learning platforms known generically as "reusable learning objects". The combination of expanding connectivity and the growing reservoir of open educational resources is a revolution. Greater connectivity allied to open educational resources could reduce the costs and expand the availability of education to the billions of people.

A good lecture should contain dynamic contents, such as animations and demonstration programmes, as well as arbitrary information from the www. On the learners side learners and other interested persons who want to retrieve courses via the internet, should not be subjected to the torture of complicated installation and operating steps.

The use of standards, the permission of any operating system and any presentation software are also required for the development of a new tele-teaching system.

The various requirements of a modern tele-lecturing system in order of their importance are given as follows –

1. Complete mapping of the classroom situation (beamer, video, voice)
2. Simple usage for the student
3. Use of standard pre-installed software
4. Platform independency
5. Simple usage for lecturer. Most desired is –

6. Integrated all in one solution
7. Usage of own equipment (e.g. Laptop)
8. Web integratable
9. Modern speed is enough for a transmission
10. Online (live, on-demand) and offline (CD, DVD, download) capable.

Electronic learning or e-learning is a general term used to refer to computer enhanced learning. It is used interchangeably in so many contexts that it is critical to be clear what one means when one speaks of 'e-learning'. In many respects, it is commonly associated with the field of advanced learning technology (alt), which deals with both the technologies and associated methodologies in learning using networked and/or multimedia technologies.

1. Many technologies can be used in e-learning, including,
2. Screen casts
3. E-portfolios
4. Electronic performance support system
5. Mp3 players with multimedia capabilities
6. Web-based teaching materials
7. Hypermedia in general
8. Multimedia cd-roms
9. Websites
10. Discussion boards
11. Collaborative software
12. E-mail
13. Blogs
14. Wiki
15. Text chat
16. Computer aided assessment

17. Educational animation
18. Simulations
19. Games
20. Learning management software
21. Electronic voting systems
22. Virtual classrooms

Features Unique to E-Learning

E-learning promises to provide a single experience that accommodates the three distinct learning styles of auditory learners, visual learners and kinesthetic learners. Other unique opportunities created by the advent and development of e-learning are more efficient training of a globally dispersed audience and reduced publishing and distribution costs as web-based training becomes a standard. In conjunction with assessing needs, e-learning can target specific needs. And by using learning style tests, e-learning can locate and target individual learning preferences.

Synchronous e-learning is self-paced. Advance learners are allowed to speed through or bypass instruction that is redundant while novices slow their own progress through content, eliminating frustration with themselves, their fellow learners and the course.

Overall Advantages of E-Learning

1. E-learning fosters interaction among students and instructors. Interaction stimulates understanding and the recall of information.
2. Accommodates different learning styles and fosters learning through a variety of activities that apply to different learning styles.
3. Fosters self-paced learning whereby students can learn at the rate they prefer.
4. Convenient for students to access any time, any place.
5. Reduces travel time and travel costs for students.

6. Encourages students to browse information through hyperlinks to sites on the worldwide web and thereby find information relevant to their personal situations.
7. Allows students to select learning materials, or to be directed to content that meets their level of knowledge, interest and what they need to know to perform more effectively in their particular activity.
8. Provides context sensitive help (electronic performance support systems) to computer users and helps them complete tasks on the fly.
9. Develops knowledge of the internet that will help learners throughout their careers.
10. Encouraging students to take responsibility for their learning and succeeding builds self knowledge and self-confidence.

Knowledge Packaging (KP)

1. Knowledge packages (KP) are the collections of learning objects described through the knowledge-packaging format interpret the rules included in them and present different knowledge routes to each learner, according to his/her profile thus facilitating personalized learning.
2. Packaging knowledge can be done in various ways. Some focus on the formation of presentation and some on the content of the message, some are graphics to deliver the message and some use text. Some present the message in listed points or in summary/abstract format. Setting an appropriate information packing format depends on a number of factors
   (a) the problem or issue being addressed
   (b) the decision-making process
   (c) the information user/stakeholder-type as well number of users
   (d) the level/scale at which the activities are taking pace
   (e) the intended effect of providing the information, and
   (f) the medium through which the information is delivered.

3. The contents in knowledge packaging could be assembled in e-content, short course or module and full courseware and short reusable learning objects. It should be based on learning objective, entry knowledge of learner, skills and preferences.

Conclusion

The rapid evolution of information and communication technologies (ICT) and the emergence of the information society create numerous new opportunities for the improvement of the quality of education. Especially the internet and www facilitate mouse-click access to enormous information repositories and learning material and services, providing an unprecedented potential for education and training. It can be argued that education has not yet realized the full potential of the information society. Even the internet is under exploited from an educational point of view both for "formal" curriculum-based, as well as in self-directed "informal", educational settings, vocational training and other learning settings. It is high time to think in a positive direction and utilize the ICT based educational components and the virtual resources effectively and efficiently especially in higher education.

19

Teachers Must Possess A Set of Requisite Technical Skills

Introduction

Flipped classrooms are shifting the way teachers provide instruction by inverting traditional teaching methods to engage students in the learning process. Using technology, lectures are moved out of the classroom and delivered online as a means to free up class time for interaction and collaboration. In order to effectively implement a flipped classroom, teachers must possess a set of requisite technical skills, conceptual knowledge and pedagogical expertise. Through this study, a web-based instructional module was developed to provide this information to prospective teachers interested in implementing a flipped classroom. Results indicated that the module was effective in delivering an overview of the required material, but could have benefitted from the inclusion of added examples of working implementations to raise the confidence level of the participants. Added support through a learning community, either in-person or online, would help to provide guidance through initiation and expand on the shared experiences of the individuals.

For years, teachers have filled the role of "sage on the stage" imparting their wisdom during allotted class time then sending work home to reinforce learned concepts with minimal or no added support (King, 1993). As a result, students were left on the receiving end of a one-way communication process that did little to promote social interaction or encourage critical thought.

Passive by nature, this model of teaching, known as the transmittal model, assumes students as empty vessels into which knowledge is poured (King, 1993). Information, once acquired, is stored without relevance and left unchanged over time. Though common, this model does little to effectively prepare today's students for a future where success relies on one's ability to think independently, solve unexpected problems and deal with complex issues. By contrast, the constructivist model presents learning as an active, social process in which learners use existing knowledge and prior experiences to build an individual understanding of new material (Brown, Collins, & Duguid, 1989). Teachers act as facilitators, guiding students through the learning process while allowing them to shape their own understanding of the instruction (Rhodes & Bellamy, 1999). By doing so,students are able to actively construct knowledge in a meaningful manner that allows them to both better understand and process the learned content. As a means to integrate the constructivist model into their classrooms, teachers are now utilizing technology to implement a blended learning method that shifts lectures out of the classroom and on to the internet in order to free up class time for collaborative activities. This inverted method, known as a flipped classroom, combines the benefits of direct instruction and active learning to engage students in the educational process. Though simple enough to understand, flipped classrooms are not quite as simple to implement due the range of technical skills, conceptual knowledge, and pedagogical expertise required to execute the varying aspects of the method. Therefore, the purpose of this instructional design project was to develop and evaluate a web-based module for teachers at a private, college-preparatory institution to effectively implement a flipped classroom in their courses.

Background

Pioneered by chemistry teachers Tom Bergman and Aaron Sams of Woodland Park High School in Colorado, flipped classrooms use technology to invert the traditional teaching environment by delivering lectures online as homework and opening up the class period for interactive learning (Tucker, 2012). Through this method, teachers record their lessons using simple video capture software, post them to the internet and assign the recordings for online viewing prior to class. By delivering the lecture beforehand, scheduled class time is made available for collaborative activities. This shift allows instructors to transition out of their role of "sage on the stage" and become facilitators, or "guides on the side" thereby allowing students to move away from being passive listeners and becoming active participants in the learning process (King, 1993). Research indicates that compared to those in traditional lecture-based classes, students in active learning environments show improved retention and better conceptual understanding of learned material (Sezer, 2011). These results are attributed to the contrasting roles of passive and active learners in the educational process. While passive learners exist solely as receivers, active learners are full participants in the process, allowing them to add to their retentive capabilities through continued self-reinforcement(Petress, 2008).Though shown to be effective once established, active learning environments are not generated spontaneously. Teachers must work to develop these environments through the use of proper motivational strategies and active promotion of social interaction. The ARCS model provides teachers with a systematic approach to design instruction that addresses the four major components affecting motivation – attention, relevance, confidence and satisfaction. Addressing these components builds intrinsic interest in the material and stimulates students' motivation to teach (Keller, 1987).In promoting social interaction, the establishment of collaborative learning communities is essential. Through these communities, the social aspects of everyday life are utilized to acquire knowledge on a given topic, thereby turning education into a natural process (Wenger, 1998). With each interaction, learning takes place in an informal environment that reduces the need for traditional lectures.

Methodology

With interest in flipped classrooms building over the last year, coverage has increased significantly, yet despite the wealth of information now available, instruction on how to start the implementation process is severely limited. As a means to fill that void, an instructional module was created to provide interested teachers with a comprehensive online resource to begin flipping their classrooms. To provide participants with the requisite technical skill, conceptual knowledge and pedagogical expertise to effectively implement a flipped classroom, a flexible web-based platform was used to accommodate the range of content being offered (Figure 1). Along with text and visual diagrams, videos were identified and presented to address the alternative learning styles of the participants as well as improve understanding by providing a new perspective on the material (Herder, Subramanian, Talukdar, Turk & Westerberg, 2002)

The module was arranged in a progressive, rolling layout that moved step by step through the implementation process. To accommodate the varying technical skills of the participants, multiple options for the creation and delivery of video were offered. In addition, three different learning strategies were presented for participants to identify the most suitable approach for their course. The instructional strategies covered in the module were the ARCS model of motivation, problem based learning method and collaborative learning approach. The instructional module can be found at http://www.kokuamai.com/test/flipped. *Technologies* The instructional module was delivered through an HTML-based web page utilizing CSS and Javascript. Videos were displayed through an embedded YouTube player dispersed throughout the module. Screen cast-o-matic and Screenr were used to capture and deliver all screencast tutorials. Survey questions were created and responses collected using Google Forms.

Population

Participants were teachers in grades 7 through 12 at a private, college preparatory institution in Honolulu. All were college educated and had a minimum of five years teaching experience. No limitations were placed on age, gender or technical skill, though all were proficient using the internet for general web browsing and to access email. Courses taught by the participants varied. Students in these courses were comfortable using the internet and had regular access to a computer with broadband connectivity outside of the classroom.

Data Collection

In lieu of traditional pre- and post-tests, a retrospective survey was used to determine the effectiveness of the instructional module. This type of survey, which requests both retrospective and current assessments of the instruction after completing the module, allows participants to maintain a consistent frame of reference when responding and limits the number of incomplete responses that can occur with pre- and post-tests (Raidl, Johnson, Gardiner, Denhem, Spain, Lanting, Jayo, Liddil, & Barron, 2004). Quantitative assessments were conducted using Likert scales to measure the effect of the Module on the technical proficiency of the participants as well as to gauge their Understanding of the conceptual and pedagogical processes. Open-ended surveys provided qualitative data to determine the module's impact on the feelings and attitudes of the participants toward implementing the learned method. Demographic data was limited to the number of years teaching, grades taught and Subjects taught. No additional personal information was collected.

Discussion

Responses indicated that the instructional module was useful for a majority of the participants. The decision to offer a broad scope of content allowed the varied participant pool to identify select areas of interest to fill their respective deficiencies. For those with little or no knowledge of flipped classrooms, the information within the module allowed them to build a strong overview of the model and provided enough of an introduction to get started with implementation. For some, the information was a little too broad. Requests for additional specificity by both beginners and advanced users indicated that the inclusion of additional resources was necessary to address their varying deficiencies. Though it would take time to identify and present the added information, the web-based platform utilized for this module could easily accommodate more content. Though examples were included in the module, an increase in the number of real life implementations presented would have helped to raise the confidence levels of participants intending to implement the method in their courses. Seeing working examples of the model in action would likely have provided answers to questions unaddressed by the module and reduced the level uncertainty with the process. To address the concerns of participants teaching less conventional subjects, ideas could have been proposed or relevant examples found to address their needs. Providing even the most basic example of a potential lesson would show these participants that the flipped classroom model is suited for all types of courses. Support beyond the module also needs to be considered. Though some participants expressed gratitude for the thoroughness of the instruction, there was still a bit of lingering hesitation as they moved into implementation. The establishment of a learning community, either online or in-person, would help beginners work through the early stages and provide guidance for more advanced users looking to expand on their initial implementations. Knowing that support is available would help to reduce the fear of uncertainty and give users the confidence to move forward on their own.

Conclusion

Flipped classrooms have the opportunity to cause a significant shift in the way instruction is delivered. Using technology, teachers are now able to provide an alternative to traditional lecture-based models by implementing a blended learning method that combines the benefits of direct instruction and active learning to engage students in the learning process The method itself, while not difficult to initiate, requires a set of technical skills, conceptual knowledge and pedagogical expertise to implement effectively. Delivering those skills through a single module is best accomplished through a broad approach that provides users with an overview of the method and gives them the proper skills and expertise to get started. To enhance their knowledge, participants must be exposed to working examples within their area of instruction to build confidence in their ability to implement the method on their own. Access to support communities should also be made available to provide guidance and expand on the learned experiences shared by their peers.

References

1. Brown, J. S., Collins, A., & Duguid, P. (1989). Situated Cognition and the Culture of Learning. Educational Researcher, 18, 32-42.
2. Herder, P., Subramanian, E., Talukdar, S., Turk, A., & Westerberg, A. (2002). The use of video-taped lectures and web-based communications in teaching: a distance teaching and cross-Atlantic collaboration experiment. European Journal of Engineering Education, 27(1), 39-48.
3. Keller, J. M. (1987). Development and use of the ARCS model of motivational design. Journal of Instructional Development, 10(3), 2 – 10.
4. King, A. (1993). From sage on the stage to guide on the side. College Teaching, 41(1),30.
5. Petress, K. (2008). What Is Meant by "Active Learning?". Education, 128(4), 566-569.Raidl, M., Johnson, S., Gardiner, K., Denhem, M., Spain, K., Lanting, R., Jayo, C.,Liddil, A., & Barron, K. (2004) Use Retrospective Surveys to Obtain Complete Data Sets and Measure Impact in Extension Programs. Journal of Extension,42(2). Retrieved from http://www.joe.org/joe/2004april/rb2.php
6. Rhodes, L. K., & Bellamy, T. (1999). Choices and consequences in the reform of teacher education. Journal of Teacher Education, 50, 17-26.
7. Salter, D., Pang, M. C., & Sharma, P. (2009). Active Tasks to Change the Use of Class Time within Outcomes Based Approach to Curriculum Design. Journal of University Teaching and Learning Practice, 6(1), 27-38.
8. Sezer, R. (2010). Pulling out All the Stops. Education, 130(3), 416-423.
9. Tucker, B. (2012) The Flipped Classroom. Education Next, 12 (1). Retrieved from http://educationnext.org/the-flipped-classroom/
10. Wenger, E. (1999). Communities of Practice: Learning, Meaning, and Identity. Cambridge University Press.

20

Teaching with Technology and Transforming Learning

Introduction

Flipped classroom is a form of blended learning in which students learn new content online by watching video lectures, usually at home and what used to be homework is now done in class with teachers offering interaction with students instead of lecturing. This is also known as backward classroom, flipped class is reverse teaching. Flipped class becomes more popular, new tools may emerge to support the out-of-class portion of the curriculum. In particular, the ongoing development of powerful mobile devices will put a wider range of rich educational resources into the hands of students, at times and places that one must convenient for them. The flipped model puts more of the responsibility for learning on the shoulders of students while giving them greater impetus to experiment. This paper briefly discuses the methods and practices of Flipped classroom teaching and its pros and cons. Key words: Activity Learning, Educational Technology, and Learning Environment

A room full of students means a room full learning strength, weakness and styles that cannot all succeed to the same degree of learning from the same instruction. Flipped class becomes more popular, new tools may emerge to support the out-of-class portion of the curriculum. In particular, the ongoing development of powerful mobile devices will put a wider range of rich educational resources into the hands of students, at times and places that one must convenient for them. Jonabam Bergman's and Aaron Sam's discover of the flipped classroom has lead to monumental success in students mastery of skill.

History

In 2004, Salman Khan began to record videos at the request of a younger cousin who felt that recorded lessons would let her skip parts she had mastered and reply parts that were troubling her Khan's model essentially provides one-to-one tutoring. Khan Academy videos are used as part of some educators "flipped teaching strategy".

In the 'The classroom Flip' (2006) Tenneson and McGlasson presented an approach for teachers considering whether to flip their classrooms and how various approaches could enhance their teaching process, along. It also explores computer course management system.

Meaning of flipped classroom

The FLIP classroom is the latest learning model, to have taken the teaching and training world by storm. Flip teaching (or flipped classroom) is a form of blended learning in which students watch lectures online and work on problem sets with other students in class. The value of a flipped class is in the repurposing of class time into a workshop where students can inquire about lecture content, test their skills in applying knowledge and interact with one another in hands on activities.

Objectives

Flipped classroom, it is an active learning model that inverts traditional lectures. Students listen to lectures on-line or through videos at their convenience before coming to class.

1. To help free up class time for collaborative learning (Blended and Participatory learning)
2. To keep large classes engaged in active learning.

How does it work?

The flipped classroom is a reverse of teaching model.

1. Before class, as homework, students review and study content materials prepared by the teacher.

2. Class time is used to practice and experience the content learned to a level of mastery under the supervised guidance of the teacher.

   The teacher serves as Tutor

3. The teacher develops videos and resources using multiple form of technology.

4. More flexibility in teaching.

Using the flipped instructional model, teachers and students can spend more time working together and dealing into complex problems. Teachers are better able to meet Common Core Standards.

Transforming learning: Flipped Vs Traditional

The purpose of flipping the classroom is to shift from passive to active learning to focus on the higher order thinking skill such as analysis, synthesis and evaluation (Bloom, 1956). In the flipped classroom the roles and expectations of students and teachers change where:

1. Students take more responsibility -they apply knowledge and skills to a range of activities using higher order thinking.

2. Significant learning opportunities can be gained through facilitating active learning, and providing timely feedback uses a variety of pedagogical strategies.

3. There is a greater focus on concept exploration, meaning making and demonstration or application of knowledge in the face to face setting.

Role of Educational Technology

Educational technologies are important features of the flipped classroom as they can be used to

1. Capture key content for students to access at their own convenience and to suit their pace of learning (e.g. lecture material readings, interactive multimedia)
2. Presenting learning materials in a variety of formats to suit different learner styles (e.g. text, videos, audio, multimedia)
3. Providing opportunities for discourse and interaction in and out of class (e.g. polling tools, discussion tools, content creation tools)
4. Convey timely information, updates and remunerations for students (e.g. micro blogging, announcement tools)
5. Provide immediate and anonymous feedback for teachers and students (e.g. quizzes, polls to signal revision points)
6. Capture date about students to analyze this progress and identify 'at risk' students (e.g. analysis)

The implications for teaching and learning

The flipped classroom constitutes a role change for instructors, who give up their front-of-the-class position in favour of a more collaborative and co-operative contribution to the teaching process.

Active learning

Active learning is a key aspect of the flipped classroom and can be applied to any learning environment from online to standard lectures or as a blend these. The aim is to promote engagement using problem solving, critical thinking and analytical skills to help prepare students for professional practice. The common active learning pedagogies are useful in teaching:

(a) Collaborative learning
(b) Enquiry based learning
(c) Problem based learning

* Case study
* Peer learning
* Project based learning

Advantages

1. Easily accessed and controlled by the learner.
2. Establishes dialogue and idea exchange between students, educators, and subject matter experts regardless of locations.

3. Class time is used for collaborative student work, experimental exercises, debate, and lab work.
4. Learn from the best sources and maintain access to challenging curriculum.
5. Enables students to access courses at higher-level institutions, allowing them to progress at their own pace.
6. Prepares students for a future as global citizens.
7. Allows students with multiple learning styles and abilities to learn at their own pace.

The Pros

1. Students have more control
2. It promotes student-centered learning and collaboration
3. Lessons and content are more accessible (provided there is tech access)
4. Access = easier for parents to see what's going on
5. It can be more efficient

The Cons

1. It can create or exacerbate a digital divide
2. It relies on preparation and trust
3. There is significant work on the front-end
4. Not naturally a test-preparation form of learning
5. Time in front of screens–instead of people and places–is increased

Conclusion

Despite these issues, the flipped classroom can still be a very effective, hands-on approach to improving student achievement and involving them in their own education. The flipped classroom model encompasses any use of using Internet technology to leverage the learning in the classroom, so that teacher can spend more time interacting with students instead of lecturing. Students spend more time working on real problems and less time sitting and listening to instruction. By providing instruction at home, parents understand the material and the method taught. Parent involvement increases.

References

1. Jerry Overmayer's FlippedClassroom.com
2. The Flipped Class: Myths vs. Realities
3. *Flip Your Classroom*, by Jonathan Bergmann and Aaron Sams
4. The Flipped Class Network
5. http://www.knewton.com/flipped-classes
6. http://www.techsmith.com/flipped-classroom

21

Use of Ict in Teaching- Learning & Evaluation

Introduction

Development in ICT has made significance impact on all spheres of human life. The impact has been rather prominent in cast of service activities such as banking, health, transportation, education and Libraries. The benefits of ICT in services can be explained in terms of economy, ease, extension and efficiency to provide their services 24- hours a day in a very cost effective manner.

This paper discusses the use of ICT in Teaching Learning of Evaluation.

1. Gurukul system of Education was in vogue in India. The main characteristics of Gurukul System were dedicated and knowledgeable teachers, individualized and learner centre teaching, and self-motivated students eager to learn. It was thought that some teachers are born but rests of them have to be given rigorous training so as to develop required competency to become an effective teacher.

2. Teachers had been and are conscious about the quality of their teaching. To enhance the quality, some teachers use teaching aids, like, charts, models-static & working, specimen, slides, etc, because teachers are given training both in preparation and use of Audio- Visual Aids. It is a known fact that majority of schools do not have appropriate teaching aids related to the school content. So teachers have no facility to use AV Aids during teaching. The use of AV Aids get further restricted due to unmotivated persons becoming teachers.
3. Programmes offered through television were produced by different State Institute of Educational Technology (SIET) in different languages. Even the Video Instructional Materials were produced and make available to teachers; still majority of schools did not make use of them.
4. The findings of researchers were in favour of programmed Learning Material (PLM),

Use of Computer

1. The lust of quality is still on. This is the age of INFORMATION dominated by the Digital Technology. The Digital Technology has influenced all aspects of human life. Education is not an exception. Now the technology will be available for the use of society.
2. At present majority of devices are based on Digital Technology. One such device is Computer. The computer is an electronic device that has the capacity to store, retrieve & Process both qualitative & quantitative information fast and accurately.

Information Technology

1. Networking of Computers gave birth to Information Technology (IT), UNESCO considered information Technology as "Scientific, technological and engineering disciplines and management techniques used in information handling and processing, their application, computers and their interaction with men and machines, and associated social economical and Cultural matters"

2. It includes micro-electronics and info-electronic based technologies incorporated in many products and production processes and increasingly affecting the service sector. It covers inter alias computers, electronic office equipment, telecommunication, industrial robot and computer controlled machine, electronic components and software products.
3. The information Technology leads to development of Websites. Government, Corporate sector, educational institutions, etc. Started uploading the information on their websites. It provides facilitates for Chat, e-mail, surfing, etc. It opens up a new source of information which increases the limitation of access to information. Prior to IT, people were using only the print material for searching the information. It limited the search. This limitation has been overcome by IT.

Information and Communication Technology

It was limited only to the textual mode of transmission of information is transmitted to the user not only in textual form but also through audio, video or any other media. Thus, the ICT = IT + Other media has opened new avenues, like, online learning, e-learning, Virtual University, e-coaching, e-education, e-journal, etc. the ICT bring more rich material in the classrooms and libraries for the teachers and students.

The ICT being the latest addition in the teaching learning process can be used both at school and higher education levels in the following areas:

1. Teaching
2. Diagnostic Testing
3. Remedial Teaching
4. Evaluation
5. Psychological Testing
6. Virtual Laboratory
7. Online Tutoring

8. Development of Reasoning & Thinking
9. Instruction Material Development

Use of ICT in Teaching

Teaching at school as well as at Higher Education level, mostly, concentrates on giving information which is not the sole objective of Teaching. Along with giving information the other objectives are:

1. Developing understanding and application of the concepts
2. Developing expression power
3. Developing reasoning and thinking power
4. Developing of judgment and decision making ability
5. Developing comprehension, speed and vocabulary
6. Developing self-concept and value clarification
7. Developing proper study habits
8. Developing tolerance and ambiguity, risk taking capacity, scientific temper, etc

With the present infrastructure, class size availability of teachers, quality of teachers, training of teachers, etc., it is difficult to achieve all the objectives.

1. At present ICT may be of some use. It is a well known fact that not a single teacher is capable of giving up to date and complete information in his own subject. The ICT can fill this gap because it can provide access to different sources of information. It will provide correct and comprehensive information in different formation with different examples. ICT provides online interaction facility. Students and teachers can exchange their ideas and views, and get clarification on any topic from different experts, practitioners, etc.
2. ICT provides flexibility to learners which are denied by the traditional process and method. Flexibility is a must for mastery learning and quality learning.
3. On INTERNET many websites are available which may be utilized by teachers and students for understanding different

concepts, improving vocabulary, developing reasoning & thinking etc, ICT can help in preparing students for SAT, GRE, TOEFL., etc.

Use of ICT in Diagnostic Testing

The common observation is that the quality of teaching in the classroom is on the decline. More and more students are depending on the private tutorial classes

The student progress can be monitored and his performance can be improved. This will develop confidence in students and may change their attitude towards the subject. It may also help in reducing the suicidal tendencies among students. Students may start enjoying learning. Further, the following are the main advantages of Computer Based Diagnostic Test. They do not require any special setting or arrangement. The only requirement is computer systems and software.

1. The student can use it even at their home if made available on school website.
2. It saves time on the part of the teacher and students.
3. The feedback is given immediately ager the test is over, which gives an intrinsic reinforcement to the student.
4. It can be update from time to time.
5. It is economical in terms of money as it requires only one time investment.

Use of ICT in Remedial Teaching

1. Once the ICT is used for diagnostic purpose, the next step is to organize Remedial Teaching Programme. The Remedial Teaching can be done by the teacher if some common mistakes are identified. It may not be feasible to organize Remedial programme for individual student. At this point, the ICT can be used for giving individual Remedial Programme. It may be online or off line.
2. The instructional material if designed specifically for meeting the individual needs of students and uploaded on the School

websites, then the ICT can be used for providing Remedial teaching programme.

Use of ICT in Evaluation

1. At present the paper pencil tests are conducted for evaluating the academic performance of students. These tests are conducted in the group setting. The content coverage in the group setting. The content coverage is poor and students cannot use them at their own. These tests are evaluated by the teachers and they may not give feedback immediately to each and every student.
2. The ICT can be used in the evaluation.
3. If used by teachers before teaching the topic, they can prepare the topic properly. Such software can be used for internal assessment. Thus, ICT can be used to improve the quality of pre as well as in-service teacher's training.

Use of ICT in Psychological Testing

1. Through research some correlates of academic achievement have been studied. Rarely this information is used by school/ college teachers. Many of them even do not know about such researchers. Even if they know, they do not make use of it at the time of forming the group for different academic activities on the basis of individual differences.
2. Even students can use them individually and can share the result with the teacher who can help the student to improve his academic performance. This digitalized psychological testing will be easy to use and economical also. Thus ICT can be used in psychological testing also.

Use of ICT in Virtual Laboratory

1. The students understand better, if they do some practical's related to the concept. It makes learning easy and interesting. Laboratory helps in developing scientific temper.
2. In short, there are many restrictions under which the students have to work in the laboratory. Now it is possible to have

Virtual laboratory. Once the Virtual Laboratory is developed, it can provide lots of freedom to students.

3. It may be made available at the door step of each and every student by uploading it on the website. Further each country can think of developing Science Website which should give access to Virtual Laboratory and it must be free of free of cost. Such a website will not only help Indian students but also can go a long way in helping students of underdeveloped and developing countries.

Use of ICT in online Tutoring

1. The digital technology has broken the boundaries among countries. Human beings do not feel and type of restriction in communicating with people across the globe the access has become easy. It is a well know fact that all students do not understand all subjects to the same extent. Some students find Mathematics, Physics, English, Chemistry, Accountancy, etc, as difficult subjects. All educational institutions do not have well equipped laboratories and qualified & competent Faculty.
2. This is how the manpower available in India can be made use of by other countries.

Use of ICT in Developing Reasoning & Thinking

1. Web Based Instruction (WBI) can be developed with the help of ICT. According to WBI Information Centre (1997), Web Based Instruction (WBI) is an innovative approach to distance learning in which computer based training (CBT) is transformed by the technologies and methodologies of the World Wide (WWW), the Internet and Intranets. WBL presents content in a structure format allowing self-directed, self-paced instruction on any topic. WBL is a media rich learning fully capable of evaluation, adaptation and remediation, all independent of computer platform.
2. Sansanwal and Nawayot (2001) defined Web Based Instruction as a hypermedia-based instructional programme that utilizes the attributes and resources of the WWW to create a

meaningful learning environment where learning is festered and supported.

3. These abilities once developing can help individual for solving the day-to-day problems. On the whole it will improve the quality of life. Thus, ICT can be used for developing WBI for facilitating Reasoning and Thinking.

Use of ICT for Developing Instructional Material

1. At present there is a shortage of qualified and competent teachers in almost all the subjects at all levels. Not only this, even the instructional material available in the print form is not of good quality.
2. Sometimes the information given in the books is also wrong. The book reading is not very enjoyable and does not help students in understanding the concepts and retaining the information.
3. There are many teachers who are well known for the specific subject. Their lectures should be digitalized and made available to all the users. It will enhance the quality of instruction in the classrooms. The teacher can use them in the classrooms and can organized discussion afterwards so that the new points can be added both by the teacher as well as the students. It will make the teaching effective, participatory and enjoyable.
4. These lectures can be uploaded on any website and students & teachers can access any lecture they like.
5. Another form of digitalized lectures is e-content. The CEC is making efforts to develop e-content material in different subjects for the benefit of diverse users. The competent teachers can develop e-content in their own areas of specialization. This has lots of potentiality to being quality in teacher education. The ICT can be used in developing Instructional Material and e-Content.

References

1. Kurtus. R. (1998). Learning through Web "http//ezinfo.ues. indiana.edu

2. Sansanwal. D.N. (2000) Information Technology and Higher Education, University New, Vol.38,No346

3. Sansanwal, D.N (2005) Institute of Education. Devi Ahilya University, Indore.

4. Sansanwal ,D.N and Dahiya, S.S (2006). C.R. College of Education, Rohteak. Haryana.

5. Sansanwal D.N and Nawayot, N. (2001) Web Based Instruction for Selected Reasoning and Thinking Skills), Institute of Education, Devi Ahilya University, Indore.

6. WBT Information Center (1997) http://www.wbtic,com/ pruner-whatiswbt.aspx

22

Effectiveness of Computer Based Multimedia Learning Material

Introduction

Performance and behavioural outcome of the student is important aspects in school education here performance refers knowledge uplifted from the course of study. Behaviour outcome refers to social behaviour like responsible co-operation. Now a day complete is using in the entire field for the various purpose. In our education computer is used for giving instruction, administration and research. CAT, programmed instruction, PSI all is innovations in educational field to improve the performance. So the researcher has as her rightly chosen the study of the relevant effectiveness of computer based multimedia learning material on performance and behaviour outcome of high school students. The present study to find out the relevant effectiveness of computer based multimedia learning material on performance and behaviour outcome in Tindivanam Town. A samples of 100 respondents selected randomly were studied. A questionnaire method of survey was used to find out the effectiveness of computer based multimedia learning material on performance and behaviour outcome. The data were collected by using questionnaire as an instrument. Primary data were collected by conducting direct structured interview using questionnaire. All the respondents were asked the same questions in the same fashion and they were informed the purpose of study. T-test, One Way ANOVA and Correlation analysis was applied to test the hypotheses. The findings and observations are the result and outcome of the interpretations made during the study of analysis. The result found that there is a significant difference between traditional method and computer method of teaching.

Multimedia refers to any computer-mediated software or interactive application that integrates text, color, graphical images, animation, audio sound, and full motion video in a single application. Multimedia learning systems consist of animation and narration, which offer a potential venue for improving student understanding. Multimedia programme is an integral part of the educational technology. As a technique, it offers a high potential in application at different stages of education for the purpose of enhancing the teaching and learning processes, as is evident from the experience of developed countries.

The integration of multimedia technology into the communication environment has the potential to transform the students from passive recipients of information to active participants in a media-rich learning process. The introduction of multimedia or any other computer-based information technology is not intended to substitute a presenter. This new technology is intended to provide the presenter with a powerful tool that can greatly enhance communication by delivering a multisensory experience. With interactive multimedia technology, a teacher can communicate with the students by means of a presentation that becomes more than message-it becomes an active, exciting experience in a multisensory environment to create a multisensory experience. Multimedia reaches users in many different ways, enabling them to retain more knowledge and increase their understanding.

There are 4 steps in learning like attention, rehearsal, encoding and retrieval. A well designed multimedia application demands the simultaneous attention of several senses through dual encoding or the process of appealing to more than one sense simultaneously. Dual encoding facilitates and enhances the rehearsal process. Multimedia helps retrieval by associating sound, text and images with the concept being presented. Using text, images, animation and sound simultaneously greatly improves the students' retention of the knowledge and directs the students' attention to classroom (Louis, 2001).

Multimedia consists of the combination of video and movie clips and sound, text and graphic files all controlled by a piece of software and a computer which is equipped with a sound card, a video card, a CD-ROM drive and speakers or headphone. Sometimes, there is also a videodisk player, which is controlled by the software.

Computer based multimedia delivers information in a variety of ways but achieves its greatest effectiveness through interaction. In the first case, music and informative knowledge combine to convey the message. In the second case, technology provides a more effective presentation wherein information, images and sounds are technically and aesthetically integrated, focusing on a single specific purpose. The ability of students to work independently and to receive instruction suited to their needs and learning styles is inherently attractive.

Review of Literature

Dalacosta et al. (2009) developed and studied the effectiveness of Multimedia **application with animated cartoons in teaching science in elementary education.** The results of the study provide evidence that the use of animated cartoons significantly increases the young students' knowledge and understanding of specific science concepts, which are normally difficult to comprehend and often cause misconceptions to them.

Jian Hu et al. (2009) investigated the effects of introducing a software program, named the Dental 3D Multimedia System (D3DM), into the education of a group of junior dental students in their preclinical practice. One group received their training program in the traditional way, unassisted by 3D technology. The second group received their training program in the traditional manner, but also used the D3DM to supplement their education. The results showed that the D3DM-assisted group achieved higher scores and also indicated that the usage of 3D multimedia PC software had a positive impact on several aspects of subjects' performance.

Kanmani and Radha (2009) studied the Effectiveness of CAI package in basic electronics teaching. There was a significant difference between the control and the experimental group students in attainment of knowledge level, understanding level, and application level objective in the gain scores. Hence, the experimental group students were better than the control group students in attainment of knowledge level, understanding level, and application level objective in the gain scores. It was inferred from the finding that the experimental treatment is effective to the students.

Korakakis et al. (2009) made a study on the "3D visualization types in multimedia applications for science learning for 8th grade students in Greece". The aim of the study was to determine whether the use of specific types of visualization (3D illustration, 3D animation, and interactive 3D animation) combined with narration and text, contributes to the learning process in science courses. The results indicated that multimedia applications with interactive 3D animations as well as with 3D animations do in fact increase the interest of students and make the material more appealing to them.

She, Hsiao-Ching and Chen, Yi-Zen (2009) examined how middle school students constructed their understanding of the mitosis and meiosis processes at a molecular level through multimedia learning materials presented in different interaction and sensory modality modes. The dependent variables included subjects' pre-test, post-test, and retention-test scores, showing their understanding of mitosis and meiosis process at molecular level. The results of the study showed that the group which used multimedia learning material has a greater amount of visual attention and consistent with their long term retained learning than the group which did not use the same. This study adds empirical evidence of a direct correlation between the length of eye fixation behavior and the depth of learning. Moreover, it provides insight into the multimedia effect on students' cognitive process through the use of eye fixation behavior evidence.

Anboucarassy (2010) studied the effectiveness of Multimedia in Teaching Biological Science to IX Standard students. The results of the study revealed that experiment group performed better than the control group due to the exposure of multimedia based learning. Thus multimedia helps the students to sustain their interest and also their retention power compared to the traditional method of teaching. The constant use of multimedia will make students understand more and achieve more in their academic achievement. Hence it was concluded that the multimedia approach is considered to be one of the best techniques for biology teaching at IX standard level.

Ponraj and Sivakumar (2010) studied the effectiveness of Computer-Assisted Instruction in Teaching Zoology in Relation to Learners' Personality. The major findings of the study indicated that achievement scores of experimental group students were higher than the control group students after the treatment.

Yusuf, Mudasiru and Afolabi, Adedeji (2010) investigated the effects of computer assisted instruction (CAI) on secondary school students' performance in biology. The findings of the study showed that the performance of students exposed to CAI either individually or cooperatively were better than their counterparts exposed to the conventional classroom instruction. Based on the research findings recommendations were made on the need to develop relevant CAI packages for teaching biology in Nigerian secondary schools.

Objectives

1. To measure behaviour and performance of high school student.
2. To assess effectiveness in performance of high school student
3. To assess effective in behaviuoral outcome of the high school student.
4. To assess effectiveness in traditional and multimedia method of teaching.
5. To find out relevant effectiveness of computer based multimedia learning material on performance and behaviour outcome.

Hypothesis of the Study

1. High school students do not differ in their average level of relevant effectiveness of computer based on multimedia learning material on performance and behaviour outcome in traditional method and multimedia teaching of entire samples.
2. Respondents do not differ in their relevant effectiveness of computer based multimedia learning material on performance and behaviour outcome in pre test on the basis of groups.
3. Respondents do not differ in their relevant effectiveness of computer based multimedia learning material on performance and behaviour outcome in pre test on the basis of type of school.
4. Respondents do not differ in their relevant effectiveness of computer based multimedia learning material on performance and behaviour outcome in pre test on the basis of parent's education.
5. Respondents do not differ in their relevant effectiveness of computer based multimedia learning material on performance and behaviour outcome in pre test on the basis of parent's income.
6. Respondents do not differ in their relevant effectiveness of computer based multimedia learning material on performance and behaviour outcome in post test on the basis of type of school.
7. Respondents do not differ in their relevant effectiveness of computer based multimedia learning material on performance and behaviour outcome in post test on the basis of parent's education.
8. Respondents do not differ in their relevant effectiveness of computer based multimedia learning material on performance and behaviour outcome in post test on the basis of parent's income.

Methodology

The methodology adopted for the study is explained in detail. The sampling technique, size of the sample, variables of the study, description of the tool used and administration of tool are elaborated.

Sampling Technique

The random sampling techniques used in the present study. The survey should cover all the aspects of the subject selected of the study others are inferred from a study of a sample group carefully selected to be representative of the total population. At time, the survey describes a limited population which is the only group under consideration. It involves a clearly defined problem and defined objectives. It requires expert and imaginative planning. Careful analysis and interpretation of the data gathered and logical and skillful reporting of the findings. There are different findings such as social surveys, market surveys. The survey method is applied to the analysis of existing social conditions including educational conditions and to the analysis of public opinion. So in this present study, the investigator has used stratified disposition random sampling method.

Sample

Samples of 100 high school students selected randomly were studied in Tindivanam Town. Out of these high schools as many as 5 higher secondary schools have been chosen by appropriate method. All the available high school students studying in each of this selected high school were chosen as sample. Stratified disposition random sampling technique has been used in the selection of the sample.

Data Collection

Primary data, required for the present research work were collected by conducting direct interviews using questionnaire. All the respondents were given sufficient information about the study. These respondents were provided with the same questionnaires. They were also informed that they have to answer in the same fashion.

Tools used for the study

Development of effectiveness of multimedia programme and Scale by the investigator. The scale for measuring the high school student's effectiveness of multimedia towards science in the study. This scale has as many as 25 statements of which 3 point scale method.

Analysis and Interpretation

Table 1

Showing the Mean, Standard deviation of relevant effectiveness of computer based multimedia learning material on performance and behaviour outcome in pre and post test of entire samples

Groups	*N*	Mean	SD	r value
Pre test	*100*	14.79	2.69	0.346**
Post test	*100*	19.30	2.86	

Hypothesis: High school students do not differ in their average level of relevant effectiveness of computer based on multimedia learning material on performance and behaviour outcome in traditional method and multimedia teaching of entire samples.

The mean and standard deviation of relevant effectiveness of computer based multimedia learning material on performance and behaviour outcome scores of entire samples are 14.79 and 2.69 in pre test and 19.30 and 2.86 in post test. The mean score of all categories are lay in between ($M \pm 1\sigma$) value. So it is concluded that average level of relevant effectiveness of computer based multimedia learning material on performance and behaviour outcome of entire samples.

Table 2

Showing the Mean, Standard deviation and t-test for relevant effectiveness of computer based multimedia learning material on performance and behaviour outcome on the basis of groups

Groups	Sample size	Mean	Standard	t-value Deviation	Level of Significance
Pre test	*100*	14.79	2.69	12.86	0.01
Post test	*100*	19.30	2.86		(Significant)

Hypothesis: *Respondents do not differ in their relevant effectiveness of computer based multimedia learning material on performance and behaviour outcome in pre test on the basis of groups.*

The calculated t-value (12.86), which is significant at 0.01 level, confirms that there is a significant difference between relevant effectiveness of computer based multimedia learning material on performance and behaviour outcome on the basis of groups. So the null hypothesis is rejected and alternate hypothesis is accepted. Therefore it is concluded that pre test and post test groups differ in their effectiveness of computer based multimedia learning material on performance and behaviour outcome.

Table 3

Showing mean, standard deviation and t-value for traditional method among the high school student on the basis of type of school

Sl. No	Type of school	Sample size	Mean	Standard Deviation	t-value	Level of Significance
1	Government	75	14.73	2.71	0.37	0.716 (Not Significant)
2	Aided	25	14.96	2.67		

Hypothesis: Respondents do not differ in their relevant effectiveness of computer based multimedia learning material on performance and behaviour outcome in pre test on the basis of type of school.

The calculated t-value (0.37), which is not significant, confirms that there is a no significant difference between relevant effectiveness of computer based multimedia learning material on performance and behaviour outcome in pre test on the basis of type of school. So the null hypothesis is accepted and alternate hypothesis is rejected. Therefore it is concluded that government and aided school groups do not differ in their pre test score.

Table 4

Showing mean, standard deviation and t-value for traditional method among the high school student on the basis of parents education

Sl. No	Parents education	Sample size	Mean	Standard Deviation	F-value	Level of Significance
1	School	86	14.82	2.75	0.58	0.560 (Not Significant)
2	Under graduate	8	14.13	2.03		
3	Post graduate	6	14.21	2.44		
	Total	**100**	**14.79**	**2.69**		

Hypothesis: Respondents do not differ in their relevant effectiveness of computer based multimedia learning material on performance and behaviour outcome in pre test on the basis of parents education.

The calculated F-value (0.58), which is not significant, confirms that there is a no significant difference between relevant effectiveness of computer based multimedia learning material on performance and behaviour outcome in pre test on the basis of parents education. So the null hypothesis is accepted and alternate hypothesis is rejected. Therefore it is concluded that different parents education students groups do not differ in their pre test score.

Table 5

Showing mean, standard deviation and t-value for traditional method among the high school student on the basis of parents income

Sl. No	Parents income	Sample size	Mean	Standard Deviation	F-value	Level of Significance
1	Below Rs.50,000	70	14.51	2.53		0.215 (Not
2	Rs.50,000 – 2,00,000	24	15.50	3.09	1.56	Significant)
3	Above Rs.2,00,000	6	16.00	2.65		
	Total	**100**	**14.79**	**2.69**		

Hypothesis: Respondents do not differ in their relevant effectiveness of computer based multimedia learning material on performance and behaviour outcome in pre test on the basis of parents income.

Table 6

Showing mean, standard deviation and t-value for multimedia method among the high school student on the basis of type of school

Sl. No	Type of school	Sample size	Mean	Standard Deviation	t-value	Level of Significance
1	Government	75	18.75	2.91	4.33	0.01
2	Aided	25	20.96	1.93		(Significant)

The calculated F-value (1.56), which is not significant, confirms that there is a no significant difference between relevant effectiveness of computer based multimedia learning material on performance and behaviour outcome in pre test on the basis of parents income. So the null hypothesis is accepted and alternate hypothesis is rejected. Therefore it is concluded that different parents income students groups do not differ in their pre test score.

Hypothesis: Respondents do not differ in their relevant effectiveness of computer based multimedia learning material on performance and behaviour outcome in post test on the basis of type of school.

The calculated t-value (4.33), which is significant at 0.01 level, confirms that there is a significant difference between relevant effectiveness of computer based multimedia learning material on performance and behaviour outcome in post test on the basis of type of school. So the null hypothesis is rejected and alternate hypothesis is accepted. Therefore it is concluded that aided school students (20.96) scored higher mean value than government school students (18.75).

Table 7

Showing mean, standard deviation and t-value for multimedia method among the high school student on the basis of parents education

Sl. No	Parents education	Sample size	Mean	Standard Deviation	F-value	Level of Significance
1	School	86	19.34	2.87	3.19	0.01
2	Under graduate	8	16.75	3.01		(Significant)
3	Post graduate	6	20.12	2.63		
	Total	**100**	**19.30**	**2.86**		

Hypothesis: Respondents do not differ in their relevant effectiveness of computer based multimedia learning material on performance and behaviour outcome in post test on the basis of parents education.

The calculated F-value (3.19), which is significant at 0.01 level, confirms that there is a significant difference between relevant effectiveness of computer based multimedia learning material on performance and behaviour outcome in post test on the basis of parents education. So the null hypothesis is rejected and alternate hypothesis is accepted. Therefore it is concluded that different parents education students groups differ in their post test score.

Table 8

Showing mean, standard deviation and t-value for multimedia method among the high school student on the basis of parents income

Sl. No	Parents education	Sample size	Mean	Standard Deviation	F-value	Level of Significance
1	Below Rs.50,000	70	19.11	2.64	3.29	0.01
2	Rs.50,000 – 2,00,000	24	20.04	3.24		(Significant)
3	Above Rs.2,00,000	6	16.00	4.58		
	Total	**100**	**19.30**	**2.86**		

Hypothesis: Respondents do not differ in their relevant effectiveness of computer based multimedia learning material on performance and behaviour outcome in post test on the basis of parents income.

The calculated F-value (3.29), which is significant at 0.01 level, confirms that there is a significant difference between relevant effectiveness of computer based multimedia learning material on performance and behaviour outcome in post test on the basis of parents income. So the null hypothesis is rejected and alternate hypothesis is accepted. Therefore it is concluded that different parents income students groups differ in their post test score.

Findings

1. High school students differ in their average level of relevant effectiveness of computer based on multimedia learning material on performance and behaviour outcome in traditional method and multimedia teaching of entire samples.
2. Respondents differ in their relevant effectiveness of computer based multimedia learning material on performance and behaviour outcome in pre test on the basis of groups.
3. Respondents do not differ in their relevant effectiveness of computer based multimedia learning material on performance and behaviour outcome in pre test on the basis of type of school.
4. Respondents do not differ in their relevant effectiveness of computer based multimedia learning material on performance

and behaviour outcome in pre test on the basis of parents education.

5. Respondents do not differ in their relevant effectiveness of computer based multimedia learning material on performance and behaviour outcome in pre test on the basis of parents income.
6. Respondents differ in their relevant effectiveness of computer based multimedia learning material on performance and behaviour outcome in post test on the basis of type of school.
7. Respondents differ in their relevant effectiveness of computer based multimedia learning material on performance and behaviour outcome in post test on the basis of parents education.
8. Respondents differ in their relevant effectiveness of computer based multimedia learning material on performance and behaviour outcome in post test on the basis of parents income.

Conclusion

In the present study, the researcher arrive the following conclusion based on the findings. In the present study, science students have relevant effectiveness of computer based multimedia learning material on performance and behaviour outcome of high school students in Tindivanam Town when compared with other students. The researcher framed objectives and hypotheses on the basis of the above context. 100 samples were selected randomly. A standard questionnaire was used to collect the relevant data. After collecting the data they were analyzed using statistical tools such as t-test and ANOVA in the both groups (pre and post test). The result concluded that the all the science students of average level of relevant effectiveness of computer based multimedia learning material on performance and behaviour outcome.

References

1. Anboucarassy, B. (2010). Effectiveness of Multimedia in Teaching Biological Science to IX Standard students. *EDUTRACKS, 9(5): 37-38.*

2. Annaraja, P., & Jenitha Rani, J. R. (2003). Development of Visual Basic based CAI package in Commerce and its effectiveness on Achievement in Commerce. *Research and Reflections on Education.*
3. Balasubramanian, N., & Jayaraman (2001). Relative Effectiveness among Different Modes of Computer Based Instruction. *Experiments in Education, 29(2): 9-13.*
4. Chang, Chun-Yen (2002). The impact of different forms of multimedia CAI on students' science achievement. *Innovations in Education and Teaching International, 39 (4): 280-88.* Retrieved March 20, 2010
5. Dalacosta, K., Kamariotaki-Paparrigopoulou, M., Palyvos, J.A., & Spyrellis, N. (2009). Multimedia application with animated cartoons for teaching science in elementary education. *Computers & Education, 52(4): 741-748.* Retrieved March 20, 2010
6. Dawson, M. E., Skinner, S., & Zeitlin, A. (2003). Rules of Engagement: Proceed with Caution when Integrating Multimedia learning Tools into Existing Course Formats. *Electronic Journal of Science Education, 7(4).* Retrieved March 21, 2010
7. Diseko, R. & Van Der Westhuizen, D. (2006). The Design and Development of a multimedia Tutorial for facilitation constructivist Learning among Nursing Science students: A Design experiment. *Proceedings of World Conference on Educational Multimedia, Hypermedia and Telecommunications 2006, pp. 493-499.* Retrieved March 20, 2010
8. Garnett, P., Hackling, M., & Oliver, R. (1997). An Interactive Multimedia Package Designed to Improve Beginning Students' Understanding of Chemical Equations. *UniServe Science News, Vol. 8, pp. 18-21.* Retrieved March 21, 2010
9. Jian Hu, Hao Yu, Jun Shao, Zhiyong Li, Jiawei Wang & Yining Wang (2009). Effects of dental 3D multimedia system on the performance of junior dental students in preclinical practice: a report from China. *Advances in Health Sciences Education, 14(1): 123 – 133.* Retrieved March 20, 2010

10. Junaidu, Sahalu (2008). Effectiveness of multimedia in learning & teaching data structures online. *Turkish Online Journal of Distance Education-TOJDE, 9(4), Article 7.* Retrieved March 21, 2010

11. Kadhiravan, S., & Suresh, V. (2001). Effect of Computer-assisted Instruction on Self-regulated Learning. *Perspective in Education, 18(3): 161-169.*

12. Kanmani, M., & Radha, M. (2009). “Effectiveness of CAI package in basic electronics teaching”, *Journal of All India Association for Educational Research, 21(1): 47-50.*

13. Korakakis, G., Pavlatou, E.A., Palyvos, J. A., & Spyrellis N. (2009). 3D visualization types in multimedia applications for science learning: A case study for 8th grade students in Greece. *Computers & Education, 52(2): 390-401.* Retrieved March 21, 2010

14. Liao, Yuen-kuang & Chen, Yu-wen (2007). The Effect of Computer Simulation Instruction on Student Learning: A Meta-analysis of Studies in Taiwan. *Journal of Information Technology and Applications, 2(2): 69-79.* Retrieved March 21, 2010

15. O’Day, Danton H. (2007). The value of Animations in Biology Teaching: A Study of Long – Term Memory Retention. *Journal of CBE - Life Science Education, 6(3): 217-223.* Retrieved March 20, 2010

16. O’Day, Danton H. (2007). The value of Animations in Biology Teaching: A Study of Long – Term Memory Retention. *Journal of CBE - Life Science Education, 6(3): 217-223.* Retrieved March 20, 2010

17. Ozmen, Haluk (2008). The influence of Computer-Assisted Instruction on students’ conceptual understanding of chemical Bonding and Attitude toward chemistry: A case for Turkey. *Computers and Education, 51(1): 423-438.* Retrieved March 21, 2010

18. Ponraj, P., & Nellaiyapen, N. O. (2008). CAI in teaching Zoology. *Research and Reflections on Education, 6(2): 18-21.*

19. Ponraj, P., & Sivakumar, R. (2010). Computer-Assisted Instruction in Zoology in Relation to Learners' Personality. *EDUTRACKS, 9(6): 34-37.*

20. Prinz, A., Bolz, M., & Findl, O. (2005). Advantage of three dimensional animated teaching over traditional surgical videos for teaching ophthalmic surgery: a randomised study. *British Journal of Ophthalmology, 89(11): 1495-1499.* Retrieved March 21, 2010

21. Pryor, Caroline R., & Bitter, Gary G. (2008). Using multimedia to teach in-service teachers: Impacts on learning, application, and retention. *Computers in Human Behavior, 24 (6): 2668-2681.* Retrieved March 20, 2010

22. Rotbain, Y., Marbach-Ad, G., & Stavy, R. (2008). Using a computer animation to teach high school molecular biology. *Journal of Science Education and Technology,* 17(1): 49 – 58. Retrieved March 21, 2010

23. Segers, E., & Verhoeven, L. (2002). Multimedia support of early literacy learning. *Computers and Education, 39(3): 207-221.* Retrieved March 20, 2010

24. She, Hsiao-Ching & Chen, Yi-Zen (2009). The impact of multimedia effect on science learning: Evidence from eye movements. *Computers & Education, 53(4): 1297-1307.* Retrieved March 20, 2010

25. Thilaka Suresh (2000). Instructional strategy change on the achievement in biotechnology and attitude towards science among higher secondary school students. *Journal of All India Association for Educational Research, 12(3 & 7): 14-19.*

26. Venkataraman, S. (2008). Relative effectiveness among selected modes of CAI in physics in relation to learner's personality. *Unpublished Doctoral Dissertation, Annamalai University. Chidambaram.*

27. Vernadakis, N., Zetou, E., Tsitskari, E., Giannousi, M., & Kioumourtzoglou, E. (2008). Student attitude and learning outcomes of multimedia computer-assisted versus traditional

instruction in basketball. *Education and Information Technologies, 13(3): 167-183.*

28. Victor, Adeosun Olufemi (2008). Relative effects of three Multi-Media Instructional Packages on Nigerian student's achievement in Social Studies. *Pakistan Journal of Social Sciences, 5 (5): 415 – 420.* Retrieved March 20, 2010

29. Yusuf, Mudasiru O., & Afolabi, Adedeji O. (2010). Effects of Computer AssistedIinstruction (CAI) on Secondary School students' performance in biology. *TOJET: The Turkish Online Journal of Educational Technology, 9(1): 62-69.* Retrieved March 21, 2010.

23

Shift in An Educator's Teaching Paradigm

Introduction

After nearly 2 years of research in blended learning, and detailed interviews with more than 30 companies, we find that blended learning is replacing "e-learning" as the next big thing. Our research finds that blended learning programs are perhaps the highest impact, lowest cost way to drive major corporate initiatives. Companies have discovered unique and powerful methodologies for selecting the "right media" to solve a given business problem. The biggest challenges companies face include technology and the change management and business processes required to roll out major programs. Results: Blended Learning solves the problem of speed, scale, and impact - and leverages e-learning where it's most appropriate, without forcing e-learning into places it does not fit. Go to article. The first generation of e-learning or Web-based learning programs focused on presenting physical classroom-based instructional content over the Internet. The experience gained from the first generation of e-learning often riddled with long sequences of "page-turner" content and point-and-click quizzes, is giving rise to the realization that a single mode of instructional delivery may not provide sufficient choices, engagement, social contact, relevance, and context needed to facilitate successful learning and performance.

One of the problems with e-learning in the early days was that learners worked on their own without any interaction with an instructor or other learners. It soon became clear that social interaction was an important ingredient in many learning situations, and that it might need to be built into some e-learning solutions. This was essentially the beginning of the concept of "blended learning". This term refers to a learning solution that incorporates a mix of online and face-to-face elements. It has been further refined to mean a learning solution that contains a mix of formats, media and experiences, comfortable with the new world of online learning. Mix and match, duck and dive: This 12th Think Tank in our series examines key questions that face learning and development professionals in every organization, In these days, various types of scientific exchange and expert reports are often held in universities to demonstrate and improve their teaching and academic level. While for the limitation of space and time, how to present all the valuable lectures to more students is the main problem. it not only can live streaming the overall audio, video media and computer desktop information but also can make recording of brilliant performance for future VOD service anywhere anytime.

Defining Blended Learning

Blended learning uses the tools of the provincial learning management system (LMS) to teach and support learning in a face-to-face class. Through blended learning, K-12 students can access high-quality course materials, course calendars, and assignments during and outside school hours. Students can also take part in face-to-face lessons and communicate with their teacher and classmates using a suite of secure online tools inside the password-protected LMS. These tools help students learn or review key concepts, stay organized, show what they have learned, submit assignments, track their achievement, and communicate with others. This suite of online secure tools includes:

Introducing Blended Learning

An experience of uncertainty for students in the United Arab Emirates The cultural dimension of Uncertainty Avoidance is analyzed in this study of an introduction to blended learning for international students. Content analysis was conducted on the survey narratives collected from three cohorts of management undergraduates in the United Arab Emirates. Interpretation of certainty with blended learning was found in: student skills with technology; student acknowledgement of course organization; and student appreciation of online feedback. Uncertainty with the introduction of blended learning was found: when membership was assigned for group work, higher quality research methods were introduced; where course structure lacked detail, increased time was required for new and different online activities. The implications of these findings are discussed, and strategies suggested for introducing blended learning to international students. The limitations of the study are considered, and a direction for future research is suggested. This is the first study on undergraduates in the Middle East for the effects of a cultural dimension when introducing blended learning. The findings increase the body of knowledge that relates to learning technology in the international business classroom.

We study the effect of one dimension, from within a culture framework, on the introduction to blended learning for business undergraduates at a university in the United Arab Emirates People are not generally aware of the tremendous impact that national culture has on their vision and interpretation of the world. Because culture colors nearly every aspect of human behavior, a working knowledge of culture and its influences can be useful to executives operating in a multicultural business environment.

Implications for K-12 Education

Restructuring the Class

One of the most difficult challenges of transforming a traditional K-12 class into a blended learning classroom requires a shift in an educator's teaching paradigm. Instead of preparing the necessary materials for the off-line setting of a traditional classroom, the blended learning K-12 teacher now must also organize and maintain the on-line, virtual classroom. The time, planning, and organization needed to restructure a K-12 blended classroom requires the educator to, in essence, plan and organize a class in two settings, which complement each other in terms of scheduling, content, lesson flow, and organization.

A blended learning classroom requires the K-12 instructor to develop teaching materials prior to the start of class. Other K-12 classroom models have also used other characteristics of blended learning for instructing students through the Web and other electronic tools. Web-enhanced campus courses, Web-centric courses, Web-courses using distance learning and campus settings, and traditional distance courses have implemented web use to certain degrees. Each category of web integration requires a varied percentage of packaged developed material, ranging from fifty to one hundred percent. (Boettcher and Conrad 1999) However, the percentage of prepared material web material in blended K-12 course ultimately depends on teacher preference, student/school technological capabilities, and other lesson dependent factors.

Like the other models of Web integration in the K-12 classroom, blended learning courses need to successfully address and incorporate four of the following components:

1. **Administration** – organization of the syllabus, increase teacher productivity/efficiency, distributing/collecting material, and scheduling duties
2. **Assessment** – providing feedback, tracking student progress, and testing opportunities
3. **Content Delivery** – communicating content through different learning styles, using multimedia, incorporating learning activities, using the Internet for the acquisition of knowledge
4. **Community** – building the classroom community through synchronous/threaded chats, providing office/help hours to communicate online

Benefits of Blended Learning

One of the more potentially impacting benefits of blended learning is in the area of student accessibility. According to Jeffrey, the ability to use the Web for the classroom has the potential to serve any student, at any time, in any place. (Jeffrey 2003) Likewise, the characteristics of blended learning also allow its K-12 students the same advantages in terms of accessibility. A blended learning's online course components could possibly minimize the accessibility concerns for the following K-12 students who cannot meet in the traditional classroom:

1. students in rural or small school districts where the proximity of the classroom is the main challenge to content/material accessibility
2. home-schooled students with instruction in subjects their parents feel unable to teach
3. handicapped or hospitalized students who cannot travel to the traditional classroom
4. expelled students who are required not to attend the traditional classroom as a consequence but still can have access to material to prevent falling behind academically
5. To provide a model to create the appropriate blend by ensuring that each ingredient, individually and collectively, adds to a meaningful learning experience.
6. Bulletproof Instructional Design:

We contend that educators may not be aware of the impact of culture, and that it is useful for an educator to recognize the influence of culture on their students. For culture will impact both the perception of the learning environment and learner's behavior. Of course this is equally true of the educator's vision and interpretation, but that is for a separate study. In the culture model, the UAE is classified within the Middle East cluster of nations, and we investigate Uncertainty Avoidance (UA) because of the high score in that region for this cultural dimension .UA is defined as "the extent to which the members of a culture feel threatened by ambiguous or unknown situations" A confidential survey to evaluate the introduction of blended learning was administered to three cohorts of students. Content analysis of collected narrative data revealed student certainty and uncertainty for the introduction of a blended learning environment. Three indicators of certainty with a blended learning environment were found:

1. student skills in the use of technology;
2. student acknowledgement of course organization; and
3. Student appreciation of online feedback. Uncertainty with the blended environment was also indicated:

Awareness about the cultural dimension of UA increased this educator's ability to diagnose potential challenges that may affect the introduction of blended learning. Some lessons learned, and changes in pedagogy are suggested as a consequence of the study. The findings add to the body of knowledge, as this is the first study to be conducted on the effect of a cultural dimension for the introduction of blended learning to There was appreciation for the organization of assignment deadlines available to students in the LMS However, data about assignments revealed increased time on task due to searching for quality sources in the virtual library Comments about time on task were found in the context of "deadlines", appearing at twice the rate in the uncertainty than the certainty classification. Keywords "research" and "sources" were associated with the less positive classification because of time and difference to the norm of searching online. Learners commented on interaction as "different" in a blended classroom to the previous experience of a more traditional class. However, the key word "difference" also revealed uncertainty with change associated with new tasks, especially where change related to traditions in exam format. An "open laptop" exam format with individual questions introduced the potential risk of failure for students. Unless students considered they had received a lot of practice, e.g. in online exam preparation or in searching for sources

There were misconceptions also about unfamiliar activities, and a desire for more information expressed With in this study of learners from a high UA culture, there was evidence of reliance on Professor feedback The professor was also expected to be flexible in expectations for the use of technology. Quotation 14 relates to student use of competence with technology, but needing flexibility in its use. A learner revealed how knowledge was attained through online group work The interpretation was that interaction is beneficial Students appreciated group work, although there was a sense of uncertainty with unfamiliar classmates To follow is a discussion about the themes that arose as implications for teaching and learning when a blended environment is introduced to students with high UA.

Discussion

The emergent themes revealed implications for changes in pedagogy to avoid uncertainty when introducing students to blended learning. These implications are contained in the final column of and are considered further in this discussion. Our study findings did not reveal student certainty or uncertainty about the shift to a more technologically supported classroom, concurring with findings related to this generation's familiarity with technology. However, as Bennett, Matron, and Kevin argue, familiarity with technological tools is not the whole debate, surrounding the introduction of learning technology for the "Next Generation", of so called "digital natives" Our research firmly places culture into the debate about learning technology/blended learning. The cultural dimension of high UA requires the international educator to consider culture and adapt blended learning to avoid potential resistance by those who are risk averse to a new learning environment.

As there is a tendency for less structure in blended learning, those from cultures who prefer more structure may perceive the environment rather vague Uncertainty manifested itself through survey narrative in students' requests for more structured learning, e.g. explicit verbal and written direction was wanted ambiguity for students, there is an opportunity to post asynchronous "diagnostic feedback", on why answers are wrong, and "prescriptive feedback", on how the answers could be improved for next time Although an educator risks student uncertainty, because of less structured pedagogy, employment preparation is of concern as more structure is considered to stifle innovation in the workplaces.

Lectures as a mode of structured instructional delivery were complemented, in this blended environment, with instructor facilitation of online group activities When the professor changes her or his role from the more traditional delivery of knowledge to become a student guide towards online material and facilitator in online group discussion and projects, it can increase uncertainty for students. The professor assigned team membership to introduce cultural diversity into online groups Hwang and Francesco 2010; Hwang, Kessler, and Francesco 2004). However, students expressed their uncertainty on this practice through less than positive survey comments. A preference was for certainty in the attitudes of familiar others, known performance, or regular decision making. However, for online discussions that carried less weight in the final grading criteria, the professor continued to assign student group members. This practice was aligned with skills needed for a global workplace, as team orientation is vital for the ability to work across boundaries, to influence people without formal authority and to lead teams composed of different cultures.

Assignments were formulated to increase knowledge about local issues. Students in this region require exposure to management in the Arab world because many will be employed in the Middle East Students were familiar with searching online through the Internet for sources to complete assignments. However, a pedagogical approach to improve research quality, through use of the virtual library, created and therefore, "seamless linking of e-learning and e-library" becomes crucial Further links to library sources were embedded in the LMS, and a research workshop was later introduced in an attempt to ameliorate UA when searching for quality regional and global sources.

A change in the exam norm caused students to exhibit uncertainty, as revealed in narrative relating to perceived unfairness and increased time on activity. Education for those with high UA must "encourage gradual acquisition of knowledge and skills practiced in a supportive environment, where mistakes are never fatal" Progressive change is suggested to reduce UA, e.g. a change to exam format, from written to electronic, followed later with other changes to exam procedure. The results agree with findings that learners from high UA cultures spend more time completing online tasks and attribute results to circumstances rather than acknowledging self-control for learning The introduction of blended learning makes necessary a longer view of time for knowledge acquisition, that is more fitting with learners from high UA cultures

Limitations and future research direction

A limitation of article length only allowed analysis of one dimension, (UA), in a culture framework to be applied to this introduction of blended learning. A further limitation is that data collected were from learners who were also taught by the survey creator. There was potential bias in data interpretation by the teacher/creator/collector. To ameliorate bias, a research colleague reviewed the results, and a future survey is planned to collect data from learners taught by others. Survey data collected in other courses, and interpreted through other cultural dimensions, will extend the value of a culture framework for blended learning.

Conclusion

The mid semester LCLC survey addressed the research question, i.e. what evidence is there of learner uncertainty or certainty on the introduction of blended learning? To investigate the introduction of blended learning, an analysis of the cultural dimension of UA was conducted. Interpretation of certainty with blended learning was found in: student skills with technology; student acknowledgement of course organization; and student appreciation of online feedback. Uncertainty with the introduction of blended learning was found: when membership was assigned for group work, higher quality research methods were introduced; where course structure lacked detail, increased time was required for new and different activities. Findings increased the international researcher's ability to interpret collected data on learner experiences within a cultural dimension . A culture framework also offers valuable insights for the educator to effectively introduce blended learning to international students.

References

1. Abdurrahman, H. & Storti, G. (2011) 'Organizational training across cultures: variations in practices and attitudes', Journal

of European Industrial Training, vol. 35, no. 1, pp. 45–70. Publisher Full Text

2. Adeoye, B. & Went ling, R. M. (2007) 'The relationship between national culture and the usability of an E-learning system', International Journal on E-learning, vol. 6, no. 1, pp. 119–146.

3. Alebaikan, R. & Troudi, S. (2011) 'Blended learning in Saudi universities: challenges and perspectives', Research in Learning Technology, [online] Available at: http://www.researchinlearningtechnology.net/index.php/rlt/article/view/10750/12370

4. Alodiedat, A. & Eyadat, Y. (2008) 'The effect of intranet use on students' achievement and self-confidence', International Management Review, vol. 4, no. 1, pp. 72–87, 109.

24

Digitally Enabled Learning Activities

A hot topic in education, Blended Learning is gaining more and more attention from teachers. As schools adopt learning platforms, teachers want to know how to use them efficiently, and are turning to blended learning approaches. Blended Learning is a tool for every teacher. Proponents of blended learning argue that by incorporating the "asynchronous internet communication technology" into courses serves to "facilitate a simultaneous independent and collaborative learning experience" and this incorporation is a major contributor to student satisfaction and success in such courses. The use of information and communication technologies has been found to improve access to as well as student attitudes towards learning.

Blended Learning

Blended learning is a formal education program in which a student learns at least in part through online delivery of content and instruction with some element of student control over time, place, path or pace. While still attending a "brick-and-mortar" school structure, face-to-face classroom methods are combined **with computer-mediated activities**.

The term **blended learning** is generally applied to the practice of using both online and in-person learning experiences when teaching students. In a blended-learning course, for example, students might attend a class taught by a teacher in a traditional classroom setting, while also independently completing online components of the course outside of the classroom. In this case, in-class time may be either replaced or supplemented by online learning experiences, and students would learn about the same topics online as they do in class—i.e., the online and in-person learning experiences would parallel and complement one another.

History of the Term

The concept of blended learning has been around for a long time, but its terminology was not firmly established until around the beginning of the 21st century. One of the earliest references to the term appears in a press release in 1999, when the interactive learning centers, an atlanta-based education business, announced its change of name to epic learning. The article mentions that "the company currently operates 220 on-line courses, but will begin offering its internet courseware using the company's blended learning methodology."

Word Usage and Context

The terms "blended," "hybrid," "technology-mediated instruction," "web-enhanced instruction," and "mixed-mode instruction" are often used interchangeably in current research literature· However, recent researchers. In the United States tend to use the term "blended learning" with more regularity.

Community

The blackboard learning management system helped develop a better feel for an online community where discussions can be held to better aid students. This virtual learning environment helps connect professors with students without physically being present, thus making this a 'virtual cafe'. Many schools use this online tool for online classes, class work, question & answer forums, and other school related works.

Also called *hybrid learning* and *mixed-mode learning*, blended-learning experiences may vary widely in design and execution from school to school. For example, blended learning may be provided in an existing school by only a few teachers or it may be the dominant learning-delivery model around which a school's academic program is designed. Online learning may be a minor component part of a classroom-based course, or video-recorded lectures, live video and text chats, and other digitally enabled learning activities may be a student's primary instructional interactions with a teacher. In some cases, students may work independently on online lessons, projects, and assignments at home or elsewhere, only periodically meeting with teachers to review their learning progress, discuss their work, ask questions, or receive assistance with difficult concepts. In other cases, students may spend their entire day in a traditional school building, but they will spend more time working online and independently than they do receiving instruction from a teacher. Again, the potential variations are numerous

Blended Education

Blended education. Hybrid learning. Flipping the classroom. Whatever one chooses to call it, this method of learning–which combines classroom and online education–is going places and making headlines along the way. While education experts continue to debate the efficacy of hybrid learning, its very existence has challenged them to re-evaluate not just technology's place in (and out of) the classroom, but also how to reach and teach students more effectively.

Definition of Blended Learning

Defining hybrid or blended education is a trickier task than one might think–opinions vary wildly but the essence is clear: hybrid education uses online technology to not just supplement, but transform and improve the learning process.

That does not mean a professor can simply start a chat room or upload lecture videos and say he is leading a hybrid classroom. According to education elements, which develop hybrid learning technologies, successful blended learning occurs when technology and teaching inform each other: material becomes dynamic when it reaches students of varying learning styles. In other words, hybrid classrooms on the internet can reach and engage students in a truly customizable way. In this scenario, online education is a game changer, not just a supplement for status quo.

Blended Learning in Action

In the course of higher education, blended or hybrid learning is a snazzy, yet relatively new tool, and not all professors use it the same way. Trends have emerged, however.

For instance, most professors in blended classrooms use some version of a course management system application to connect with students online. Blackboard and moodle are perhaps two of the best known applications used today. Through platforms like these, students can access video of lectures, track assignments and progress, interact with professors and peers, and review other supporting materials, like PowerPoint presentations or scholarly articles.

How Hybrid Classrooms Are Redefining Education

In a traditional classroom, instructors use class time to lecture and disseminate support materials. Students then review these materials and complete any assignments at home, on their own time. With some luck, teachers will review those assignments in class the following day, or at least host office hours so that they can field questions and offer support. "Flipping" defies these conventions. In this method, teachers and professors use online media to deliver notes, lectures and related course materials. Students review these materials at home and at their own pace. Classroom periods are then transformed into hands-on work periods where the teacher–who will have already delivered his or her lecture digitally–is free to field questions, engage class-wide discussions or offer other means of support.

Does Blended Learning Work?

Not all students learn the same way. This is not a particularly novel concept, but it is an important one. Students never outgrow their learning styles, so why do traditional college classrooms fail to engage all of them?

This is blended learning's real strength: it transforms a largely transmissive method of teaching–say, a professor lecturing for what feels like an eternity–into a truly interactive one. It sounds ideal on paper, but does it work? A 2010 meta-analysis published by the U.S department of education suggests it does. According to the report, students exposed to both face-to-face and online education were more successful than students entirely in one camp or the other.

Is there a Catch?

Of course, no educational model is one-size-fits-all, and some hybrid classrooms are probably more effective than others. Teachers must be committed to and well trained in blended and hybrid education and its technologies, and students must have a clear understanding of what is expected of them in this new environment. As blended learning becomes more common, schools and professors will likely understand and implement it better. Yet even now, early in the game, blended education shows promise, making this an exciting time to be a student.

New Resource Provides Guidance on Delivering Blended Learning

Blended learning, recently one of the most popular methods in education, is more than just a superficial trend. According to Gallup's recently released "State Of America's Schools" report, blended learning holds incredible potential for increased student outcomes as well as increased capacity for student and teacher engagement—a major driver of achievement, says the report.

By incorporating information technology into class projects, communication between lecturers and part-time students was improved, and students were able to better evaluate their understanding of course material via the use of "computer-based qualitative and quantitative assessment modules" in a study by Alexander and Mckenzie (1998).

Time-Saving and Pedagogical Benefits for Teachers

"Blended learning is performing or conducting your teaching in a combined classroom - the combination of the physical classroom and the virtual classroom. You use the traditional space and then you add something to it," he explains. "Most teachers look at the two elements of blended learning - the physical and virtual classroom - as two separate things. But the value is in the combination, the combined classroom."

Reform

Over the past decade, digital- and online-learning options have become more popular and more widely used in public schools, although many schools have been slow or reluctant to adopt new technologies for number of complex reasons, ranging from inadequate funding, technologies, and computing networks to general organizational recalcitrance and resistance to change.

Conclusion

Blended learning is not so much an innovation as it is a natural by-product of the digital domain creeping into physical boundaries. As digital and social media become more and more prevalent in the life of learners, it was only a matter of time before learning became "blended" by necessity. That said, there's a bit more to blend and "hybrid" learning than throwing in a little digital learning. However, "as new technologies and online learning continue to grow in popularity, implementation and training for teachers and administrators have unfortunately remained a stumbling block—until now".

25

Learning without Limit

Introduction

Grouping by ability holds children back argues head teacher **Alison Peacock**, whose school went from failing to outstanding when the whole staff worked to ban limiting beliefs about fixed abilities and fixed futures and became a listening school. Learning without Limits College Preparatory Elementary School helps students to become leaders who are passionate, curious and equipped with the skills and knowledge needed for high achievement. We build on the knowledge students bring with them to school and monitor their progress closely to ensure success's convincing. "The style and language used by the authors make the book readable and therefore a book that practicing teachers can actively use as a guide to improve their practice...it is amply demonstrated that teaching can and should be an activity whose primary focus is to enhance students' learning capacity and not limit it." The authors analyze these case studies and identify the key concept of transformability as a distinguishing feature of these teachers' approach. They construct a model of pedagogy based on transformability: the mind-set that children's futures as learners are not pre-determined, and that teachers can help to strengthen and ultimately transform young people's capacity to learn through the choices they make.

Literature and research spanning many decades have drawn attention to the damaging effects of ability labeling on young people's learning and life chances. Yet determinist beliefs about ability continue to have currency in schools. Indeed, the idea that child are born with a given amount of intellectual power, has gained renewed strength and legitimacy in recent years. Government-sponsored initiatives to raise standards and improve practice in schools have placed particular emphasis upon the need to differentiate by 'ability'. Teachers are expected to make explicit in their schemes of work how this differentiation is to be achieved.

"Creating Learning without Limits' takes on one of the most important issues in education today. In the last decade schools in England have taken a path towards putting all children into boxes, attaching are capable of achieving. This book shows the possibility of a different educational path, one in which all students are encouraged to achieve the greatest they can. Importantly the book also documents ways in which courageous teachers can do this - promoting fair and engaging learning environments for all students. This is a must-read for educators, policy makers and parents alike".

"College is a place where a professor's Lecture notes go straight to the student's lecture notes, without passing through the brains of either" - EDWIN EMORY SLOSSON

Learning without Limits College Preparatory Elementary School is the right fit for you and your child if you are looking for a school that treats you like a partner. At **LWL,** we are dedicated to seeing all children make dramatic progress. Students who attend **LWL** agree to make one another feel loved and cared about. When students feel a sense of belonging at school, they are able to give their full attention to their work and when they do that, they learn without limits! The Learning without Limits project is dedicated to developing approaches to teaching and learning that do not rely on determinist beliefs about ability. The purpose of the project is to support the development of approaches to education that allow every child's learning to flourish, free from such externally imposed limits.

'Special Educational Needs'

Learning without Limits website The big idea of 'transformability' and the four practical, pedagogical principles outlined above have been used to inform and inspire whole-school development; to support teachers in initial training and courses of further professional development; they have helped to inform a foundation degree course in Higher Education and a local authority support service dedicated to fostering the inclusion of children deemed to have 'special educational needs'.

Small Group Section

1. Support small, closed study groups within a larger course:
2. On-campus class announcements
3. Closed forums
4. Notes and note-taking tools
5. Instructor access to grades for the students in the section
6. Facilitate closer interactions between instructors, TAs and students
7. While benefiting from the richness of interaction in a larger community

Flexibility in Course Structure

1. High-quality online content
2. Produced locally or adopted from another institution
3. High-touch interaction with local instructor
4. Active learning, problem solving, personal attention to students
5. Self-selected level of guidance – Multi-campus or multi-section enrollment
6. Attention from instructor.

Learning without Limits

1. A study of teachers for leadership of learning

2. Everybody
3. Co-agency
4. Trust

Digital Learning

Park Manor has developed an Accelerated Learning Framework to help us effectively integrate digital learning into our curriculum in ways that accelerates the learning of all of our students. The Accelerated Learning Framework was just published in Michael Fullan's latest book "Stratosphere 'students as seekers, users and creators of their own knowledge'.

Learning Theories and Styles: (Six-Element Typology of Teaching Tasks and Objectives)

(1) Attention,

(2) Perception and recall,

(3) Organization and sequencing,

(4) Instruction and feedback,

(5) Learner participation, and

(6) Higher-order thinking and concept formation.

The following media and modes are considered because they are common and familiar, and also because they constitute the tools most available to online teachers, trainers, and learners:

(1) Print and text,

(2) Still graphics and illustrations,

(3) Sound and music,

(4) Video and moving graphics, and

(5) Multimedia.

Perception and Recall

Perception requires that the learner selectively focus on and make sense of stimulation in the environment, including the learner's own internal states and responses (thoughts, feelings, and physiological states). Recall involves the ability to remember and make use of relevant prior learning, as well as of the learning acquired in a given situation.

1. **Organization affects perception;** that is, events, ideas, words, concepts, and other stimuli that are not organized in some meaningful way are more difficult to understand and remember than those that are.
2. **Perception and recall can be aided by comparison and contrast;** similarity and grouping also assist recall.
3. **Presentations that focus on differences are distinguished better by learners** and their contents may be easier to recall.
4. **Modeling and demonstrations** can result in learning. While learners eventually must become active in the process of acquiring skills and knowledge, students can also learn while watching.
5. **Repetition and review** increase learning up to a point. (Depth of understanding, breadth of proficiency)

Concept Formation and Higher-order Thinking

The learning of concepts or principles is often intended to be part of a process leading to engagement with other, related concepts. In formulations such as **Gagne's (1970),** below, the learning sequence is hierarchical, and as the learner moves up the sequence, more complex orders of reasoning are required:

1. **Signal learning**; involuntary responses; for example, the startle response, or removing a hand from heat.
2. **stimulus-response learning**; involuntary, selective responses; for example, signaling in response to a specific cue, or imitating an action.
3. **motor-chain learning**; performing a sequence of actions in a certain order; for example, dancing, parallel parking, or replacing a light bulb.

4. **verbal association or verbal chaining**; reciting correct responses to cues; for example, singing the lyrics of a song, reciting the alphabet, or translating a word from one language to another.
5. **Multiple discrimination**; responding differently to similar stimuli; for example, distinguishing individual
6. **concept learning**; responding to new stimuli according to properties they share with previously encountered stimuli, or comparing properties of phenomena.
7. **Principle learning**; putting two or more concepts together in a relationship (without necessarily being able to explain the underlying rule governing the relationship)
8. **problem-solving**; recalling previously learned principles and using them in combination to achieve a goal.

Media, Modes, and Learning

Technologies, as channels through which modes (symbols acting as stimuli) pass, differ in the responses they evoke in users. For example, text is a mode of presentation. Print-on-paper is one possible medium (channel) for text, but there are others: a computer monitor, an overhead projection, a television screen, film (moving or still), etc. In this way, media may help to reduce "transactional distance" in learning the communication gap or psychological distance between participants which may open in a teaching-learning situation.

Human and Technology-based Teaching

Technologies differ from one another, and instruction delivered online differs from human-delivered teaching. Consider, in the analysis, the effects of media-based training compared with training done by stand-up, face-to-face instructors.

Media Characteristics and Impacts on Learning

Five types of media, from print to multimedia defined as **"the integration of video, audio, graphics, and data within a single computer workstation";** The argument here is that, as technologies continue to evolve, it will be increasingly possible, technically, to use ever more complex media, including multimedia as defined above, to deliver instruction.

Print and Text

There is no medium more ubiquitous than print, and no mode more familiar than text in its many forms. Print was part of the first teaching machine—the book—and books was the first mass-produced commodity. Print has been the dominant medium to date in distance education, and distance students have traditionally spent most of their time studying alone, often using print materials only. The chief strengths of print and text have traditionally included:

- **Cost**—reports that print is one of the lowest cost one-way technologies.
- **Flexibility and robustness**—print scores highest on these features.
- **Portability** and ease of production—with desktop publishing hardware and software, printing has become enormously simpler and its quality much higher. In addition, costs can be reduced with local production.
- In **stability** organization and sequencing are positively affected, since text-only printed and online materials can be reorganized and resequenced with relative ease by cut-and-paste operations, using word-processors and HTML editors.
- **Convenience,** familiarity, and economy—instruction and feedback are facilitated by the medium's familiarity, as, for adept learners and the highly literate, are higher-order thinking and concept formation.

Video and Animation

According to **Roberts (1998),** video adds a sense of direct involvement and physical presence among geographically dispersed learners.

- provides quality learning opportunities
- Gives distant sites live, interactive learning opportunities.

- Enables the delivery of global expertise to remote learners.
- Eliminates or reduces travel time and time away from jobs and family.

The advantages in actual practice of various forms of video continue to be debated. In some studies, animation has been shown to result in a reduction in study time, **"suggesting that animation results in more efficient learning"** with learning effects persisting over time, when compared with **"highly imaginative examples and illustrations,"** the advantages of animated simulations were less obvious in concluded from his analysis that "any widespread belief in the superiority of animation over non-animated instruction within the context of computer-based instruction is at odds with the research" According to **Roberts (1998),** critical issues in the delivery of video-based training include those listed below.

1. Proper training of instructors.
2. User self-consciousness.
3. Integration of other media into video presentations.
4. Optimum length of sessions and size of groups.
5. Session variety.
6. Technical design and support.
7. Professional quality visual elements.

Obviously, video delivery is complex, potentially costly, and of uncertain benefit for some teaching tasks over simpler, more economical media. A clear pedagogic and business case is obviously needed for its use. Despite these potential limitations and weaknesses, multimedia also has potential strengths when used appropriately. Advantages of multimedia for instruction:

The Internet

As noted at the outset of this chapter, **"online learning"** almost always denotes learning **"on the Internet."** The Internet offers both advantages and challenges to educators and trainers. The advantages arise from the Internet's enormous capacity to link participants with information and with each other. But problems with navigation, structure, interactivity, complexity, security, and sheer consumption of time must be addressed.

The Internet is potentially a powerful linking and communication vehicle. Two related Internet-based media show particular instructional promise for those with the skill and discipline to use them well, especially in relation to organization and sequencing challenges presented by the Internet: **hypermedia and hypertext**. Hypermedia is the linking of multimedia documents, while hypertext is the linking of words or phrases to other words or phrases in the same or another document. Internet delivery may be hyperlinked or linear.

Conclusion

Online learning is still in its early infancy. There are many outstanding, and, in some cases, vexing issues: costs are declining, but still limit widespread access; many users (teachers, trainers and learners) feel they do not have all the skills they need to make mature use of online learning's potential; administrators and policy-makers often overstate the likely impacts of going online and the relation of learning outcomes to technology use, for specific populations and in particular circumstances, has not been clearly identified, and is not well understood. Although these realities prove that there must be evolution before online learning can be seen as mature, at the same time there are promising signs. Finally, in-service training is increasingly available to potential users. Whether online learning follows this path or not, it has a good chance to grow because online access to information—wired or wireless, structured or user-driven—and interaction using various computer-based technologies are established social and economic realities.

References

1. Bates, A. W. (1988). Technology for distance education: A 10-year prospective. Open Learning, 3(3), 3-12.
2. Bates, A. W. (1995). Technology, open learning and distance education. New York: Rutledge.

3. Bates, A. W., Harri ngton, R., Gilmore, D., & van Sorest, C. (1992). Compressed video and video-conferencing in open and distance learning: A guide to current developments. Unpublished manuscript, The Open Learning Agency, Burnaby, BC.

4. Bloom, B. S. (1976). Human characteristics and school learning. Toronto: McGraw-Hill.

5. Bloom, B. S. (1984, June-July). The 2-sigma problem: The search for methods of group instruction as effective as one-to-one tutoring. Educational Researcher, 4-16.

26

Awareness of Flipped Classroom Among International School Teachers

Introduction

With the rise of technology, teachers organize their classrooms in innovative ways. Flipped classroom is one such innovative technique that encourages students to view online videos for the content normally taught in the class and use class time to collaborate in discussions and activities with peer and teachers. In India it is general notion that international schools have the best smart classes, multimedia and computers and emphasis will be laid on training the teachers in using the technology effectively. These schools shift from blackboards to white boards, and the students have access to advanced technologies. Using flipped classrooms teacher centric method has become discussion centric. As there is a buzz about flipped classroom among educators and teachers, this study was carried out to find the awareness of flipped classroom among international school teachers. The sample was 192 teachers with six international schools from the three southernmost districts of Tamilnadu namely Tirunelveli, Kanyakumari and Tuticorin using purposive sampling method. Questionnaire was given to all the teachers and an unstructured interview was conducted with teachers who were aware of flipped technique. The results revealed that only 8% of the teachers were aware of flipped classroom and fewer practiced it. Nearly half the population of the teachers who were ware unaware of this technique expressed willingness to learn about it, and the beliefs and perceptions of those remaining were against it. As nowadays students spend a lot of time with technology, it will be easy to engage these students with flipped learning technique. Administrative and technical support will help teachers use this innovation effectively.

Education is one field that is continuously changing adapting the growing needs of students. As their learning habits change with newer technologies, education must adapt to match those learning habits. As s digital natives spend more time playing video games, surfing the Internet, using smart phones and watching television, etc., education is forced to integrate these technologies. Computers are potentially useful tools that teachers can employ to involve students in novel learning experiences that promote active, inquiry-based learning. Instructional multimedia engages more of the senses that require more skills than just the ability to read, addressing different learning styles and serves the needs of diverse student populations (Snowden, 2012). Computer-based instruction can offer teachers the flexibility to individualize instruction and meet the needs of students who differ in motivation or ability. When traditional classroom is conducive to memorization of content, technology-rich classrooms use constructivist approach to improve students' real-world skills including composing questions, producing hypothesis, and tackling new problems intelligently (Salomon, 2002).

Lage, Platt and Treglia (2000) introduced the idea of using technology to 'flip' a traditional classroom environment. In this method, also known as inverted classroom or reverse classroom, students watch video lectures at home and complete what has traditionally been known as homework in class under the guidance of the instructor. The flipped classroom is an educational technique that consists of two parts: interactive group learning activities inside the classroom, and direct computer-based individual instruction outside the classroom. Students move from being the product of teaching to the center of learning, where they are actively involved in knowledge formation through opportunities to participate in and evaluate their learning in a manner that is personally meaningful. Bloom (1984) observed that the continuous feedback and correction students receive during one-on-one interactions significantly improves learning and achievement. Focusing on Bloom's findings, teachers have been trying to integrate one-to-one interactions with their students in the classroom. The Flipped Learning model relegates the lecture portion of the traditional classroom to the outside, and allows teachers guide students in the integration and application of the content in class.

Students of this generation have different cognitive skills than the previous generations and are very good at multitasking (Green & McNeese, 2007) and their experience with technology, induces them to get immediate feedback for work (Gee, 2003; Neto, 2001).A s the focus on integrating technology into learning increases, interest in Flipped Learning will likely continue to grow. There is a considerable amount of buzz in academic circles at all levels, focused around the flipped classroom. These appear mainly as newspaper articles in academically oriented issue (The Hindu, Sep. 2, 2013). The Flip teaching models are being incorporated by teachers of all subjects, for students of all ages. This mode of learning is now slowly making inroads into teaching and training in India.

Objectives

(i) To find the awareness of flipped classroom among teachers working in international schools.

(ii) To find if the teachers who are aware of flipped classroom implement it in teaching.

Materials and Methods

To meet the objectives of the study, the investigator collected information by constructing a survey questionnaire and personal interviews. The questionnaire comprised fifteen Yes/No questions with a tick mark response. The intention of constructing the questionnaire was that, doing a speak up survey was difficult. As the questions were focused on individual perceptions for qualitative research.

The population of this study was the teachers working in six international schools in the three southern most districts of Tamilnadu. The purposive sampling technique was used to select the subjects. All the subjects, 192 teachers after having been informed about the objectives and protocol of the study, gave their consent and participated in the study. After carrying out the survey in each school the investigator had an in depth unstructured interview with the teachers who were aware of flipped classroom. The selected demographics were sex, native place, subject handling, years of experience, classes handling, and number of schools taught earlier.

Limitations

Due to time constraint the study was limited to the teachers working in international schools in three districts. The study was confined to international schools taking into consideration that these schools extend a global level education incorporating new technologies in teaching and learning.

Results

Of the 192 teachers surveyed, only 8% were aware of flipped classroom for teaching science and language subjects. These teachers came to know about this method via friends, newspapers and the Internet. From the interview with the teachers, the investigator concluded that there is a controversial conception about the effectiveness of flipped classroom and its implementation in Indian schools. The teachers in international schools using flipped classroom strongly believe that expertise in computer technology is not a prerequisite to addition. The highlight of this study was that an international school in the southernmost tip of Tamilnadu, in a rural area, implements flipped classroom vigorously and effectively for students from grade 3- 10, what the counterparts in urban areas failed to do, thanks to the scope for accessibility to technology.

Though the remaining 92% of teachers were unaware of flipped classroom, they still actively used technologies like smart class, video lessons, online clips and multimedia for teaching and evaluation. Flipped classroom is successfully used in other countries, in all levels of education. But the teachers working in the international schools where the study was carried out were not even unaware of flipped classroom. After the survey nearly 40% of these teachers were interested to know about flipped classroom and wished to attend workshops and seminars on flipped class.

Interpretation

From the survey it was noted that half the percentage of the teachers who knew about flipped classroom were not confident in practicing it as they thought it was time consuming and laborious. Flipped classroom was not simple to implement that required a range of technical skills, conceptual knowledge and pedagogical expertise. These teachers directed students to use textbooks and other websites for reference in working out assignments and for preparation of the topic for next day. Their opinion on technology failure - power, software and internet connectivity denies the reliability of flipped classroom, and is consistent with the study by

(De Gennaro, 2008). Teachers not using flipped classroom justified their attitude stating that barriers like resources, time consumption, technical support, and the lack of overall support from administration thwart them from using it. This perception of teachers was noted in the studies by (Lim & Cha, 2008; Lowther etal 2008). Though negligible number of teachers under survey used flipped classroom method, and they strongly agreed that students prefer flipped method to other techniques, they didn't give any definite answer for student achievement.

Of the surveyed schools, administrators wanted their teachers who were unaware of flipped classroom to interact with the investigator, after the survey. The following issues emerged in the interface. Less than half the population of these teachers was curious to know about flipped classroom and was ready to attend workshops if organized. Their beliefs and readiness would make them feel comfortable in using this technology in future. The remaining teachers in this group who used technology to a nominal level in teaching, using more interactive and discussion based means of content delivery perceived flipped teaching no way better than the methods they use. Parents' opposition in permitting the students to use internet unmonitored and putting more responsibility on the students for learning supported the teachers view. The teachers rationalized their stand by listing out the negative factors in this in flipped method namely accountability for students watching the lectures, time taken to prepare and the opposition from working parents. They believe that flip method will be more beneficial for higher level education and can be successfully applied only by a technological skilled person. This is consistent with the studies carried by Sandolz & Reilly (2004) and Snowden (2012).

Discussion and implications

A good number of teachers were optimistic in learning flipped method. They should be given hands-on experience to make them comfortable with new technology before implementation. Now more than ever, students spend a majority of their waking hours using some sort of technology. All the teachers surveyed agreed that students prefer technology integrated teaching to traditional methods. Despite decreases in the cost of technology and improved access to hardware and software, implementation in the classroom lags behind expectations. The schools which have access to the latest technology, does not always improve technology integration by teachers (Lim & Chai, 2008). Teachers who integrated technology in teaching were interested to try flipped classroom if they could receive technical support. If timely, on-site, competent technical assistance is provided by the school administration teachers can effectively utilize technology (Byron & Bingham, 2001). The international school in the rural area which used flipped classroom in teaching in my study, was content about the resources, but required more technical training. A reasonable number of teachers were uninterested even in knowing about flipped classroom, many be because they lack the necessary knowledge and skills to successfully integrate technology (Eteokleous, 2008). Implementing new technology like flipped classroom in teaching depend on teachers belief and readiness. This can be achieved only by gradually replacing their beliefs with more relevant beliefs shaped by experiences in an altered context. Continued professional development programmes should be provided to the teachers by the administration to better prepare teachers to increase the frequency and intensity of technology implementation, which could perhaps yield greater and more consistent improvement in student teaching (Lowther et al., 2008). If the method is used with a proper design, including built-in support, some of the initial concerns of the teachers interviewed for this study can be dispelled. The non cooperating attitude from parents in using internet at home was pointed as a barrier to the teachers in integrating technology into learning.

As cited in a study by Lowther (2008), this study also revealed that the teacher readiness is a contributing factor to the technology integration in the classroom. Cited as an influencing factor in many studies on education; teachers who were not interested in using flipped classroom indicated resources, time constraint and technical support as major barriers (Bergman & Sams, 2012). This is a concern that must be addressed by school administration, if technology integration is a priority for schools. Teachers must be given time to incorporate new technologies, in addition to being given time to learn and receive proper training on the technologies. The teachers who already fill their class-time with student-teacher interaction, discussion, and activities certainly would not see the benefit of adding a lecture component through homework (Ronchetti, 2010). Some of the teachers surveyed thought that a few students who are not ready or capable of being responsible for their own learning, make it difficult to apply flipped method to the whole class. Some of the concerns by teacher using flipped classroom method were built-in supports and accountability including instant feedback mechanisms and interactive quizzes and worksheets. Proper training on the tested flipped classroom method might prove beneficial for those teachers with a desire to use the method. The flipped learning model provides that bridge to a learner-centered classroom environment, thereby enabling deeper learning (Bergmann & Sams, 2012) that educators are seeking. More qualitative and quantitative research needs to be done to identify how the potential of the model can be maximized.

Delimitations

Although this study has provided insight into the awareness of flipped classroom among teachers with international schools, as it was carried out in the southern three districts of Tamilnadu, generalization of findings is limited.

Conclusion

The educational community would say that the role of a teacher is being forced to change because there is no need for the teacher to be the bearer of all information. Now content is easily accessible and readily available thanks to technology. The developments in technology also change the role of a teacher by allowing him or her to challenge students in different ways, providing them with skills and experience, teaching them to be a life-long learner rather than simply teaching them the content in their subject area. Using technology, teachers are now able to provide an alternative to traditional lecture-based models by implementing a blended learning method that combines the benefits of direct instruction and active learning to engage students in the learning process. In India the schools of 'high standards' instruct teaching through video classes and conferences, online clips, digital classroom and multimedia presentations. If the teachers in these schools are made familiar with flipped classroom concept and are trained to acquire this skill, they get more time to address the needs of individual students and enable more active and engaged learning. According to research, as students spend majority of the day using some sort of technology, they are more active as learners and are less tolerant of passive learning situations, such as lectures. These schools can let the parents know about the advantages of flipped classroom and the ways to render support to their wards.

It is true that the Flipped Learning model is not the only way to facilitate good teaching, but flipped classrooms have the opportunity to cause a significant shift in the way instruction is delivered. Whether the flipped method is viewed as beneficial by a teacher or not, all teachers should recognize the need for differentiation. Every classroom is filled with a variety of different students who come from different backgrounds, have different learning styles, and different needs. Teaching methods like flipped classroom ensure that a teacher reaches more students, while keeping their interest by refusing to allow the classroom to be predictable.

References

1. Bergmann, J. & Sams, A. (2012). *Flip Your Classroom: Reach Every Student in Every Class Every Day.* International Society for Technology in Education.
2. Bloom, B. S. (1984). The 2 sigma problem: The search for methods of group instruction as effective as one-to-one tutoring. *Educational Researcher, 13(6),* 4-16.
3. Byron, E., & Bingham, M. (2001). *Factors influencing the effective use of technology for teaching and learning: Lessons learned from the SEIR-Tec intensive site schools.* Retrieved from http://www.seirtec.org/publications/lessons.pdf
4. DeGennaro, D. (2008, Fall2008). Learning designs: An analysis of youth-initiated technology use. *Journal of Research on Technology in Education,* 41(1), 1-20.
5. Eteokleous, N. (2008). Evaluating computer technology integration in a centralized school system. *Computers& Education,* 51(2), 669-686.
6. Gee, J. (2003) *What video games have to teach us about learning and literacy.* New York: Palgrave MacMillan.
7. Green, M., & McNeese, M. (2007, January). Using edutainment software to enhance online learning. *International Journal on E-Learning,* 6(1), 5-16.
8. Lage, M. J., Platt, G. J., & Treglia, M. (2000). Inverting the classroom: A gateway to creating an inclusive learning environment. *Journal of Economic Education,* 31(1), 30-43.
9. Lim, C., & Chai, C. (2008). Teachers' pedagogical beliefs and their planning and conduct of computer-mediated classroom

lessons. *British Journal of Educational Technology*, 39(5), 807-828.

10. Lowther, D., Inan, F., Daniel Strahl, J., & Ross, S. (2008). Does technology integration “work” when key barriers are removed?. *Educational Media International*, 45(3), 195-213.
11. Neto, A. (2001). Virtual worlds, real minds: An investigation about children, video games and cognition. Proceedings of the Society for Information Technology and Teacher Education International Conference 2001, 1, 3143- 3146.
12. Ronchetti, M. M. (2010). Using video lectures to make teaching more interactive. *International Journal of Emerging Technologies in Learning*, 5(2), 45-48.
13. Sandholtz, J., & Reilly, B. (2004). *Teachers, not technicians: Rethinking technical expectations for teachers.* Teachers College Record, 106(3), 487-512.
14. Salomon, G. (2002). Technology and pedagogy: Why don’t we see the promise revolution?.*Educational Technology*, 42(2), 71-75.
15. Snowden E.K. (2012). Teachers perceptions of the flipped classroom: Using video lectures online to regular traditional class lectures. University of Texas.

27

Goal of Learning Environment of Tomorrow

Introduction

Architects and educators will work together to understand key principles of teaching and designing innovative K–12 learning environments. Explore the challenges of designing spaces that enable personalized learning for students, support social and emotional development for both adults and children, better engage families and communities with schools, and include new media and information technology.

The ultimate goal is to promote systematic design thinking that will cause a paradigm shift in the learning environments of today and tomorrow. Participants are not required to have computer programming skills, but must have 1) a commitment to working in a virtual team and 2) the motivation to help people learn better. All of us have been involved in the learning process at some point in our lives; in this course we invite educators, school leaders, researchers, students, parents, entrepreneurs, computer programmers, illustrators, interface designers, and all those who are interested in working together, to create a new learning environment.

The Learning Environment for Tomorrow program engaged architects and educators from around the world in understanding key principles of teaching and designing innovative K–12 learning environments Architects and educators will work together to understand key principles of teaching and designing innovative K–12 learning environments. Explore the challenges of designing spaces that enable personalized learning for students, support social and emotional development for both adults and children, better engage families and communities with schools, and include new media and information technology.

The "Learningland" team was committed to the dramatic transformation of an aging existing building because it represents the majority of the learning spaces most schools currently operate. The team intends to take the insights gained from the institute and the workshop an initiate change in their communities.

Overview of Learning Environment for Tomorrow

Learning Environments for Tomorrow will explore four key themes emerging as defining elements of 21st century education: collaboration; technology; engagement; and sustainability. Through a research-based understanding of current and emerging best practices, participants will work with Harvard faculty and leading practitioners to envision how school buildings can most effectively support learning in the coming decade and beyond.

Working in teams you will apply your combined understanding to a school-redesign case study and develop provocative prototypes. You will answer questions such as: What is the core 21st century learning goals and programmatic features of this school? What are the guiding design principles that will drive decision-making? What might be the core design patterns and diagrams that would best represent how the goals will be realized?

To support the exploration of these themes, the program will engage participants through a variety of formats, including interactive plenary sessions, small-group discussions and project design teams.

Goal of Learning Environment

The goal of Learning Environments for Tomorrow is to provoke and collectively explore interdisciplinary insights on two overarching questions:

1. What are the principles of effective pedagogy and design for the coming decade?
2. How can new visions of learning environments be shaped by the latest research and practices in learning theory, emerging technologies, environmental sustainability, child/adult collaboration and community engagement?

In answering these questions, the program aims to achieve the following learning objectives:

1. Understand the principles of effective pedagogy and design for the coming decade
2. Learn the latest thinking in the areas of learning theory, child/adult collaboration, student and community engagement, social media technologies and environmental sustainability
3. Speculate on the modes of creativity and productivity which education will need to address in the coming decade
4. Consider the implications that the areas noted above have on designing effective learning environments
5. Critique learning environments and educational facilities that are seen as models of effective design
6. Develop planning and design strategies for facilities that serve a broad set of stakeholders—from students, teachers and administrators to the communities in which they are based

Designing a New Learning Environment

What constitutes learning in the 21st century? Should reading, watching, memorizing facts, and then taking exams be the only way to learn? Or could technology (used effectively) make learning more interactive, collaborative, and constructive? Could learning be more engaging and fun? We construct, access, visualize, and share information and knowledge in very different ways than we did decades ago. The amount and types of information created, shared, and critiqued every day is growing exponentially, and many skills required in today's working environment are not taught in formal school systems. In this more complex and highly-connected world, we need new training and competency development—we need to design a new learning environment.

The ultimate goal is to promote systematic design thinking that will cause a paradigm shift in the learning environments of today and tomorrow. Participants are not required to have computer programming skills, but must have 1) a commitment to working in a virtual team and 2) the motivation to help people learn better. All of us have been involved in the learning process at some point in our lives; in this course we invite educators, school leaders, researchers, students, parents, entrepreneurs, computer programmers, illustrators, interface designers, and all those who are interested in working together, to create a new learning environment.

Students will be able to

1. Identify advantages, disadvantages, limitations, and potentials of at least 10 interactive learning models and solutions.
2. Describe how online communication, collaboration, and visualization technology play a role in the behavioral, cognitive, constructivist, and social dimensions of learning.
3. Describe the major components and processes involved in development of interactive education systems.
4. Communicate rationales of learning technology design approaches through team-oriented collaborations.
5. Evaluate the value of ideas, principles, and techniques used in educational media or systems.

Designing Tomorrow's Learning Environment

To use creativity and collaboration to design a learning environment for the education of residents and fellows in settings that provide high-quality patient care; to apply the key themes of innovation in education; increasing clinical efficiency and quality in settings where residents learn; and advancing educational assessment through the use of the six general competencies; and through attendee consensus select a few pragmatic interventions with a high likelihood of success in immediate improvement in the learning environment.

This study provides an opportunity for individuals in graduate medical education - program directors, designated institutional officials, faculty and other leaders and experts - to explore the attributes of a high-performing learning environment. Invited key note presentations on relevant themes will be followed by design sessions that will harness participants' creativity in a collaborative, facilitated setting to develop concrete recommendations to improve the current settings for physician education, and to plan for excellence and innovation in tomorrow's learning environment.

Conclusion

This study will allow for initial design and refinements to produce concrete recommendations for the learning environment of the future. Participants also will learn about and discuss current best practices in the learning environment for adoption and adaptation in their programs and institutions.

Reference

1. Dudek, M. (2000), Architecture of Schools: The New Learning Environments, Architectural Press, Oxford.
2. Mononen-Aaltonen, M. (1998), "A Learning Environment - A Euphemism for Instruction or a Potential for Dialogue?", Media Education Publication, 8
3. Aldridge, J.M. & Fraser, B.J. (2000). A cross-cultural study of classroom learning environments in Australia and Taiwan. Learning Environments Research.

28

Learning is A Tool to Manifest the Perfection

Learning is a never end up process. Learning is a never ending process. Learning is life oriented. The language we speak, the habits we acquire, the skills we develop, the Transformations we bring about, the revolution we create and the culture we emanate all are the result of learning. Learning causes changes in behavior of an individual. Such changes in behavior occur due to practice and experience, growth and maturity which are relatively independent of activity. A relatively permanent change in behavior which occurs as a result of activity, training, practice or experience is defined as learning by pedagogists and psychologists. Learning should be profitable to human being for his progress and prosperity and useful to his society. Any learning should be purposive. It must be multiple and integrative. Though for the sake of learning, we compartmentalize learning as verbal learning, perceptual learning, motor learning, conceptual learning, problem solving learning, life – oriented learning, and emotional learning. Really speaking learning is blended to make an all – round developed personality is life in an individual. This is blended learning.

Art of learning

Learning is not something to be given. It is to be gained by self – experience. Learning is not confined with the classroom. Learning is universal and all beings learn. We learn from all living and non living things around us. Every object in the world around us tends to teach us something. And we are bound to learn from them.

Learning cannot be uniform though universal. It differs due to individual differences in perception, interest, aptitude, attitude, intelligence and personality. To some extent, heredity and environment play a significant role in learning. In this world of complexity, specialization in learning, though is insisted, cannot make one suitable to the growing globalized world. Blending different aspects such as stress management, leadership, quality, team spirit, mutual respect, sociality, equality, brother hood, fraternity, liberty, moral and social values so on and so forth should capture apt place in the process of learning.

Learning different aspects needs many internal and external factors as learning is a mean to make one's internal external. Learning is a tool to manifest the perfection already in man. Learning should not simply stuff a man or a woman with facts and figures or scores of information about an object, place or a person, it should enable one to behave and perform in an excellent and effective manner in any situation. For that mere bookish learning will be inadequate and inappropriate. Bookish learning should be co-opted with and blended with life oriented learning. For this, motivation, need maturation and urge should be felt or provided to the individual learning will be easier if the field of learning suits to one's aptitude and attitude.

Present Learning

Mostly our present learning is directed to two categories. 1. Bread winning learning and 2. Learning for obtaining a degree. The present education system is so designed that it could produce literates for executing some administrative systems or salaried class. It has no provision for producing real man who is the need of the hour. Learning should be aimed at man – making and character – building such learning can develop noble ideals as love for the nation, alleviation of poverty and literacy, producing a society of equality, honesty, justice, love, mutual respect for each other and peace and prosperous and pleasant living. Learning should help one to carry over of experiences derived from a learning situation to the learning of another task.

Real aim & Learning

The real aim of learning is to create a pleasant, peaceful, prosperous progressive and purposeful life in this universe. Our learning should enable us to abolish any conflicts- social, mental and emotional from the human race and establish love, affinity, peace, mercy, sympathy, service and sacrifice for the rest of the world.

Value education, Vocational education, cultural education, social education, environmental education, citizenship education, peace education, moral education, human rights and duties education and human resource management education should be blended with the present learning system. Learning should make one a universal being instead of an individual. Learning should develop values in one, for values are the integral part of personal philosophy of life which include our aims, ideals, manners of thinking and principles by which human world guides our behavior and conducts our affairs. The values blended with our learning are answers to the why and how questions in life. Values are our susceptive reactions to the world around us. They guide and mould our behavior.

Objective and Blended Learning

Learning should be blended with the ways of developing personal, social, family, cultural, democratic, institutional and moral values which in turn breed truth, beauty, aesthetics, goodness, gentleness, peace, bliss, happiness and above all worldly friendliness. Think truly and thy thoughts shall be worlds' famine feed, speak truly and each world of thane shall be a fruitful seed, live truly and thy life shall be a great and noble need, said Horatius Bonar. Unless learning is not blended with great value like truth, the health of the world cannot be maintained.

Learning should enlighten us to keep our environment pure and immaculate. Happiness depends on external environment which kindle or ignite real happiness. The fruit of learning too is kindling or igniting happy, healthy, harmonious and heft society. Learning should not stop with learning scientific and technical know-how to make one's life comfortable and convenient. But it must be blended with great virtues like hospitality, respecting one another, helping tendency, care, sacrifice, service, humanitarianism, tolerance unity, secularism, spirituality, problem-solving, peace and simplicity.

Bringing closer the human mind rather than the distance of the nations

Our present curriculum includes scientific and technological advancement around the world, the industrial development, researches on space, earth and health and hygiene. It makes one learn to invent or discover novel things to make human life pleasant and prosperous. But in real sense, the modern scientific gadgets have reduced distance between nations, continents and planets. But they have failed to bring human minds closer to each other. Learning has not assimilated human ideals but annihilated human relations. Everywhere we see destruction of human life due to wars, violations, extremism and hatred. Our learning has made us hate each other instead of love each other. Division in many forms instead of unity among the human race is the result of our learning. Instead of bookish learning, practical learning, peace and value learning, cultural and moral learning should be blended to create a real future happy and healthy generations.

Curriculum for blended learning

Special curriculum for blended learning right from the primary education level should be devised with the help of educationalist, moralists, religious giants, social activists, philosophers, teachers and psychologists and if possible with due student representations. Mere intellectuals are not necessary for making the world really peaceful, we need learned people with intelligence, discipline, moral values, patriotic fervor, sociability and simplicity for making the world fit for the ensuing generations to lead a happy, healthy, harmonious peaceful, prosperous, pleasant merry and meaningful life.

Methodology

1. An expert committee consisting of experts in the field of education, economy, culture, yoga, intellectual development, medicine, religious, health and hygiene and psychology may be constituted to frame a new curriculum right from primary to the higher education for blended (education) learning.
2. A periodical exchange programme between the universities in and around the world may be organized to study the functioning of blended learning programmes organized there and implement the topics suitable to our student community and national environment.
3. Faculty members and students may be sent to different institutions to discuss the usefulness of blended learning at different levels and enforce the scheme to all the institutions.
4. Novel methods of evaluations of the quality of blended learning instead of old and obsolete examination system may be suggested to assess the quality of students undergoing blended learning.

Conclusion

As we know education is the all-round drawing out the best in body mind and spirit and the manifestations of perfection already in man, it is absolutely necessary to introduce drastic changes in learning to produce good, suitable, skilful, intelligent energetic, enthusiastic, effective, excellent, erudite, problem solving and troubleshooting personality who feels emotional, moral and social responsibility to develop his own status and the status of the nation in the years to come. It is the right time to make the necessary reforms and researches for renaissance in learning process in our nation to make our children suitable to face the globalization, urbanization and liberalization policies of the world.

29

Assistance of Innovative Educational Technologies

Introduction

As per the words of Graham, C.R. (2005) blended learning is a blending of different learning methods, techniques and resources and applying them in an interactively meaningful environment. Learners should have easy access to different learning resources in order to apply the knowledge and skills they learn under the supervision and support of the teacher inside and outside the classroom. This approach will combine face-to face instruction with computer-mediated instruction. It also applies science or IT activities with the assistance of innovative educational technologies using computer, cellular or I-Phones, Sky TV channels and other electronic media. Purnima Valiathan (2002) has defined blended learning as "The term blended learning is used to describe a solution that combines several different delivery methods, such as collaboration software, Web-based courses, EPSS, and knowledge management practices. Blended learning also in used to describe learning that mixes various event-based activities, including face-to-face classrooms, live e-learning and self-paced instruction".

Blended learning combines face to face learning with on-line learning to provide the most efficient and effective instructional experience by combining delivery modalities, for example a teacher with more class room enrollment may choose the computer mediated or online elements of instruction, another teacher who in concerned about slow learners may choose face to face interaction where motivation can be infused through gesture voice and communication. The other teacher who would like to have the best of both methods can combine both of these modes by starting with a class room discussion, having some activities, web based course ware, text based job, conference calls, and so on, which may impart a holistic learning experience to the learner.

So blended learning may be considered as "The right mix of various media to maximize learning experience with minimum utility of resources to ensure optimum realization of educational objectives, by making the perfect blend of informational technology and instructional technology"

One-Up with Blended Learning

Among the electronic instructional strategies blended learning is fast picking up with the following benefits.

1. It addresses the different learning styles and multiple methods of information delivery to reinforce the lesson.
2. It offers improved pedagogy as it increases the level of active learning strategies, peer to peer learning strategies and learner centered strategies.
3. Boundless information in the World Wide Web can be accessed instantly: social interaction in relatively more in blended learning than e-learning.
4. For self motivated adult learners in offers the benefits of self regulatory learning and ease of revision.

Elements of Blended learning

As per the learners demand and expected learning outcomes the blended learning experience in designed by the experts. Bersin and

Associates (2004) have identified the following elements related to blended learning.

1. Instructor led lecture / training
2. Webinars
3. Web-based Courseware
4. Simulations
5. CD – ROM based courseware
6. Rapid e-learning courseware
7. Internet delivered videos
8. Electronic performance support system
9. Offline videos
10. Video conference
11. Collaboration system (chat room, discussion board.)
12. Conference calls
13. Job aids
14. Workbooks
15. Books
16. On the job exercise

Variants of Blended Learning

Along with the traditional lecture the course designer will use a combination of collaborative and individual activities with different media types depending on the content of the material Bersin(2004) has suggested two models of blended learning.

(i) Program flow model : and

(ii) Core – Spoke model.

These two are theoretical models in the primitive level.

Making the Right Mix

The success of blend largely depends on the right mix of the elements it posses. A good blend should provide optimum role of live interaction. It should also provide a wide choice to learners as per their self regulatory perception. It is essential to provide a good support and training model and should keep the cultural components also in mind. A blend which makes the right balance between innovations and mass utility as well as which bridge the digital divide will be the successful blended learning model.

Blended Learning for Instructional implementation

The models suggested by Bersin and Associates (2004) are reviewed and customized so that it can be used in the present context in the teaching learning process. In program flow model the activities are blended chronologically as per the nature of the topic and by the wisdom of the course designer. I show the general instructional sequence of the pogramme flow model of blending for both non-technical and technical mode of blend.

In this model in overview session the instructor can give overview either as traditional class room interaction if it is non-technical lends or through webinar if it is a technical blend. In self-paced learning activity the learner can pick books in non-technical blend and in technical blend one can go for e-books, electronic performance support system (EPSS). Query session may contain face to face and e-mail in non-technical and technical mode respectively. And demonstration will have live demo, and simulation in non-technical mode and web meeting in technical mode. Whereas collaborative session will contain role playing and chat for respective modes. Finally feedback closing session may have traditional class room in case of non-technical mode webinar or mail in case of technical mode.

In Core-Spoke model the activities are blended in a non-chronological order that is a central activity or activities surrounded by supporting activities as shown in Fig. 2 which can be used at any time during the course. In this model also the nature of the topic and the course designer finalize the activities. But the learner is at his liberty to select the sequence of activities he would like to go about.

In this model the activities CD-ROM based course ware, off-line videos, books and e-books are off-line activities. Remaining activities can be considered as on-line activities, which may be either instructors led or peer alone activities.

Suitability of Program Flow Model

This model blends the activities in the chronological order and the flow is in progressive building of cognitive structure and activities. The blend can be of either traditional or technical components. By virtue of its scaffolding of cognitive structure in a sequential order the model is best suitable for Reflectors and Theorist type of learners. As per B.S Warrier (2006) Peter Honey and Alan Munford have categorized that Reflector learners learn better when they are given an opportunity to review what has happened and think about what they have learned. Likewise Theorists are the type of learners who are structured in situations with clear purpose who do things by knowing the principles of concepts. So this model is suitable for pedagogical learning activities at school level.

Suitability of Core-Spoke Model

This model follows the non-chronological order where the learner is at his liberty with spokes activities. But in most of the cases it is suggested to have the class room activity as the core either in face to face or virtual mode. So this model will be suitable for activists and pragmatists type of learners. According to B.S. Warrior (2006) peter Honey and Alan Munford have categorized that activists learn better when given new experiences, problems and opportunities and who less likely to listen to lectures and explanation. Like Wise pragmatist learners are those who obviously like the topic to put into action and look forward to try new techniques to save time or something else. So this model will be apt for pedagogical learning activities at higher education level.

Challenges Ahead

1. Negative attitude towards new technology among the instructors and learners.
2. Cost of many on-line components is high.
3. Lot of e-content in various topics should be developed.
4. Bandwidth needed for the fast access of internet should be improved.
5. Server with better capacity needed for congestion free learning.

6. Developing adequate technological and human resources.
7. Developing adequate contingency plan in case of technical problem.

Conclusion

"Blended learning is the right mix of various media to maximize learning experience with minimum utility or resources to ensure optimum realization of educational objectives, by making the perfect blend of informational technology and instructional technology". Among these two models discussed, program flow model is suitable for Pedagogical learning activities at school level and Core-spoke model will be apt for pedagogical learning activities at higher education level. In this global village digital technologies are becoming the integral part of day-to-day life and in near future blended learning will be synonymous with learning.

Reference

1. Aycock, A, Garnham, C, and Kaleta, R. (2002). Lessons Learned from the Hybrid Course Project. *Teaching with Technology Today,* v6, n6, March 2002.
2. Bersin, J. (2004). *The blended learning book: Best practices, proven methodologies, and lessons learned.* San Francisco: Pfeiffer.
3. Bonk, C.J. & Graham, C.R. (2004). *Hand book of blended learning, Global Perspectives, local designs.* San Francisco: Pfeiffer Publishing.
4. Kurtus, R.(2004). Blended Learning http:// www.school–for–champions. com/e-learning/blended. htm. retrieved on 22nd Dec 2008.
5. Mohanasundaram, K & Sivkumar, A. (2010). Blended Learning: A New Horizon. University News, Vol.48. No.03, P-1-4.
6. Talawar, M.S & Pradeep Kumar, T. (2009). *Podcasting : A new trend of web-based technology in education. University News,* Vol. 47, No.30, P-13-15.

7. Valiathan, P.(2002).*"Blended learning Models"*ASTD learning Circuits, 2002

8. Warrier,B.S.(2006).*"Theperfect'blendedlearning"* www.thehindu.com/thehindu/edii'2006/05/08/stories/2006050800250700. htm Retrieved on 6m December 2006.

30

Success Factors for Blended Learning

Blended learning involves of concern: technology and education blended learning, which blends face-to-face learning and online learning, is becoming an attractive model in higher education as new innovative information technologies are becoming increasingly available. However, just blending face-to-face learning with information technologies cannot provide effective teaching and efficient solutions for learning. The rapid growth in the use of learning technology, particularly the use of the web based technologies and communications have offered educator with many more opportunities to investigate the most suitable learning environments for their students learning styles.

Introduction

Blended learning acording to the innosight institute is a formal education program in which a student learns atleast in par through the online delivery of content and instruction, with some element of student control over time, place, path, and / or pace and atleast in part at a supervised brick – and – mortar location away from home[1] compered to high – access environments, which simply provide devices for students, blended learning includes an international shift to online instructional delivery for a portion of the day in order to boost learning and operational productivity

Blended learning

There are many definitions of blended learning, but the most common is that which recognizes some combination of virtual and physical environments for example, Graham (2006), who describes the convergence of face-to-face settings, which are characterized by synchronous and human interaction, and Information and communication technology (ICT) based settings, which are asynchronous, and text-based and where humans operate independently. Mason and Rennie (2006) extend this definition to including "other combinations of technologies, locations or pedagogical approaches" (p.12) and Garrison & Vaughan (2008) define blended learning as "the thoughtful fusion of face-to-face and online learning experiences" (p. 5) emphasizing the need for reflection on traditional approaches and for redesigning learning and teaching in this new terrain. Littlejohn and Pegler (2006) also recommend a different approach that they term 'blended e-learning'. This is a useful approach because it changes the focus in learning design by shifting the emphasis from simply considering the face-to-face and online environments to that of considering the design issues of (1) introducing e-learning and (2) the process of blending.

As Garrison and Kanuka (2004) commented, this combination of classroom and online settings has simplicity, but there is also a complexity to the concept which is evident in the wide variety of settings, diversity of the student population and consequent learning designs. Different blends of technology and pedagogy have been documented in both campus-based and distance programmes (Stacey and Gerbic, 2006). The advent of new learning technologies, for example, podcasting and vodcasting, internet based audio and video communication, e-portfolios and social networking tools including blogs and wikis create new blending potentials. The cultural diversity of the student population and the technology rich experiences of some Net Generation students raise further issues for blended learning design. Complexity is also evident in the extent to which

ICT has been incorporated or embedded within courses. Some writers (for example, Vaughan, 2007) argue that mere supplementation of a face-to-face course with online learning is not blended learning whereas others (Littlejohn and Pegler, 2006) prefer to talk about 'strong' and 'weak' (p.29) blends to indicate a continuum across significant to very small amounts of e- learning.

In the professional development context, the blend of technologies with face-to –face interaction is a means by which a community of practice is established. The notion of a community of practice, developed well in the writing of Wenger (1998, 1999) and defined by him as those "groups of people who share a concern, a set of problems, or a passion about a topic, and who deepen their knowledge and expertise in this area by interacting on an ongoing basis" (Wenger, McDermott & Snyder, 2002, p 4) has been extended with online communication to enable learning in the workplace through a blend of face-to- face and technological interaction (Stacey, Smith & Barty, 2004). Informal communities of practice and formal communities of learning with an online resource base of web resources and case studies are the basis of much effective institutional professional development. Garrison and Vaughan (2008), in particular, promote a blended faculty *Community of Inquiry* which combines face-to face workshops, where personal relationships can be established, with a sustainable online community for critical reflection and discussion of practice.

Definitions

1. "Blended learning is the *effective* combination of different modes of delivery, models of teaching and styles of learning. Blended learning combines online with face-to-face learning. The goal of blended learning is to provide the most efficient and effective instruction experience by combining delivery modalities".
2. "the thoughtful integration of classroom face-to-face learning experiences with online learning experiences" (Garrison & Kanuka, 2004)

3. "A pedagogical approach that combines the effectiveness & socialization opportunities of the classroom with the technologically enhanced active learning possibilities of the online environment" (Dziuban, Hartman & Moskal, 2004).

Characteristics of Blended Learning

1. BL is a convergence of two "archetypal" learning environments: face to face and fully online
2. BL recognises strengths and weaknesses in both environments and attempts to **merge the strengths** to **provide more engaged learning experiences** for students
3. In blended courses human-human interaction and learner-material interaction both typically play strong roles, though to different degrees
4. Thus, different **modes of student engagement** are discernible...

Factors that promote successful blended learning

The literature on blended learning is dominated by insider accounts of its introduction in campus-based courses, generally using a learning management system and often including online discussions. These reports are often highly descriptive and factors that might promote successful blended learning are often hidden in the form of concluding observations, and recommendations and rarely identified more explicitly. The recommendations that follow are grouped under four headings which have been developed from the emergent literature, where there is an overall emphasis on pedagogic factors.

Institutional success factors

1. Blended learning models should be developed that respond to local, community or organizational needs rather than using a generic approach (Sharpe, Benfield, Robert and Francis (2006). However, Mason and Rennie (2006) advocate putting the learners' needs first, ahead of the context or the biases of the teacher in making such choices.

2. It is important that the institutional building blocks are in place including organizational readiness, sufficient technical resources, motivated faculty, good communication and feedback channels with students (Tabor, 2007).
3. There is room for staff to develop their own meanings for blended learning, currently poorly defined to include face-to-face classes and active learning and build commitment to the concept (Sharpe, Benfield, Robert and Francis (2006).
4. Blended learning should be introduced as a scholarly and transformative redesign process within the institution, that rebuilds the course rather than simply adding on technology (Sharpe, Benfield, Robert and Francis, 2006: Littlejohn and Pegler, 2007; Garrison and Vaughan, 2008).
5. There should be institutional practice of carrying out regular evaluations and publishing the results (Sharpe, Benfield, Robert and Francis, 2006).

Regarding teachers

1. The importance of, and need for, continuing professional development for teachers with sufficient time for development should be acknowledged (Vaughan, 2007).
2. Ongoing pedagogical and technical support through membership of a blended community of practice is a proven model that sustains such teacher innovation (Garrison and Vaughan, 2008).
3. The importance of dealing with teachers' fears of loss of control, lower student feedback grades and general uneasiness about the impact of online learning on classroom relationships should be considered (Vaughan, 2007).
4. The impact on teachers' workloads must be taken into account. Littlejohn and Pegler (2006) indentify the costliness in terms of both institutional and teacher investment and suggest the creation of shareable and reusable digital resources in an effort to ensure that blended learning is sustainable.

Regarding students

1. Students' learning maturity and readiness for blending learning with its demands for independent learning must be considered (Tabor, 2007).
2. Student expectations, especially their ideas that fewer face-to-face classes mean less work and the need to develop more responsibility for their learning and time management skills must be taken into account (Vaughan, 2007; Tabor, 2007).
3. Consistent and transparent communication around the new expectations is needed in order to help students understand the blended learning process (Sharpe, Benfield, Robert and Francis (2006).

Components of Blended Learning

The concept of blended learning describes environments where there are carefully planned levels of both face to face and technology mediated communication. The specific number of these types of communication can be selected to suit the learning setting.

The E-Modules combine a knowledge/theoretical component with a practical component, which consists of case studies, real-life scenarios, practical examples from the day-to-day work of the institutions and exercises in order to make the topics covered more tangible and easily accessible for the students. The e-learning tool has a user-friendly interface giving the students the possibility to control the learning process by providing information on the content of each chapter in the form of a brief description of the topics covered, a definition of the learning targets at the beginning of every chapter and information on what parts of the modules were already covered as well as offering a wide number of exercises to apply the newly acquired knowledge. In addition to the main pages, the modules also contain so-called "nice to know pages" which complement the main pages by providing additional, more in-depth information to certain aspects of the topics covered. The "nice-to-know-pages" comprise relevant articles from the Treaties, tables, pictures, graphics, maps, biographical notes, etc. It is of crucial importance for an online learning system to provide tools for self-assessment of the progress made and self-evaluation. The E-Modules offer such tools in the form of a system of page tests and chapter tests which allow the students to determine the level of knowledge and skills acquired so far as well as the areas that require further work. The test system of the E-Modules consists of multiple choice questions as well as open answer questions, and feedback is received automatically after the test has been submitted. In order to support the constant self-evaluation process, the tests can be repeated unlimited number of times. In addition, the students can choose to complete the modules with a face-to- face exam in Brussels and receive a respective certificate. As a preparation for this final exam, the students have the possibility to complete comprehensive online tests on every module, which simulate the face-to-face exam in Brussels.

Face-to-face training

The second component of the blended learning approach of the IES is the face-to-face training, which takes place in the form of three-day intensive training sessions. The face-to-face training sessions cover the most important topics of the E-Modules, but in a more intense and in-depth manner and are used to complement the online learning process. In addition, the in-house training contains further topics not addressed at length in the modules like the cosmetology procedures, interest representation and lobbying, alternatives to the so-called community method, etc. As the E-Modules, the IES training concept promotes a balanced approach, where theory and practice complement each other to facilitate the learning experience, and, therefore, accomplished academics and practitioners conduct the in-house training. Every topic is covered in a comprehensive manner with the use of practical examples, case studies, dossiers, etc. The aim of the in-house training sessions is not the one-way transmittance of knowledge, but the creation of an atmosphere for the facilitation of a dialogue with the students. The presentations on every topic are supplemented by comprehensive study materials and additional literature. The number of participants for each training session is limited so that the learning process can take place in a small group of students (between 10 and 12) in order to create a "learning community" feeling and facilitate interaction and debate between the group members on the one hand and the students and the teacher on the other hand. Experience shows that small groups are much more effective in pedagogical terms, regarding the learning outcome and the creation of a group identity. Moreover, the added value of these training sessions is not only the transmittance of knowledge, but also the motivation of students, who otherwise work on their own and feel growing isolation in the online working environment as well as the exchange of learning experiences and information. The face-to-face environment is the opportunity for all students to take part actively in the debate so crucial for teaching social sciences and to receive answers to questions they have encountered while studying the subject matter.

Blended Learning – A Review

The recent literature review exhibits two trends in blended learning definitions and research: **(1) educational-focus and (2) technological-focus**. For example, in an educational-focused manner Bliuc, Goodyear and Ellis (2007) define blended learning as "learning activities that involve a systematic combination of co-present (f2f) interactions and technologically-mediated interactions between students, teachers and learning resources" In contrast, in a technological-focused manner Allan (2007) describes blended learning as "the use of different internet-based tools including chat rooms, discussion groups, Podcasts and self-assessment tools to support a traditional course" In the last decade, much of the blended learning research has been devoted to technological-centred design and development rather than taking an educational- focus (Alavi, 1994; Liu, Abdulmataleb and Georganas, 2003; Arriaga, Alami, and Arriaga, 2003; Barker, 2006; Amelung, Piotrowski and Rosner, 2007; Fong, Kwan and Wang, 2008). To use Brabazon's (2007) term, "technology in education" highlights technologies that were designed, developed and used in education - technology is the primary focal point in the research and practice.Blended learning is the combination of different instructional technologies such as **media, learning tasks, and types of events** to produce the best possible training program for a specific audience. Blended learning programs utilize varied forms of e-learning, which may be complemented with instructor-led approaches via face-to-face settings or computer-conferencing formats. Blended learning design should be driven by learner needs.

Helmer (2003) states: "Not only is the sheer number of possible delivery methods now slightly baffling. But the breadth and diversity of experiences on offer constitutes a formidable challenge to the imagination of designers, and also threatens to take many learners well out of their comfort zones."

Conclusion

As our scenarios illustrated, blended learning provides flexibility in learning for both students and teachers. Integration of the virtual and physical landscapes enable both teachers and students to become learners but this is most effective when there is institutional support through provision of professional learning and the opportunity for redesigning courses for the most appropriate blend. For Blended Learning to be effective, all the questions about why we are blending, what we are blending and to what effect we wish to blend must be effectively and accurately answered for the blend to be a successful and sustainable one.

References

1. Alvarez, S. (2005). Blended learning solutions. In B. Hoffman (Ed.), *Encyclopedia of Educational Technology.* Retrieved April 25, 2006.
2. Helmer, J. (2003). EPIC Think Tank: Blended Learning Design. Retrieved from:
3. Stacey, E., & Gerbic, P. (2007). Teaching for blended learning - Research perspectives from on-campus and distance students. *Educational and Information Technologies, 12*(3), 165-174.
4. Garrison, R., & Vaughan, H. (2008). *Blended learning in higher education:Framework, principles and guidelines.* San Francisco: Jossey-Bass.

5. Graham, C. (2006). Blended learning systems. Definitions, current trends and future directions. In C. Bonk & C. Graham (Eds.), *The handbook of blended learning: Global perspectives, local designs*. San Francisco: John Wiley and Sons.

6. Bliuc, A., Goodyear, P., & Ellis, R. (2007). Research focus and methodological choices in studies into students' experiences of blended learning. *Internet and Higher Education, 10*, 231-244.

31

Teaching Methodology of Flipped Classroom

Flipping the classroom' is a pedagogical concept and method that replaces the standard lecture-in-class format with opportunities for students to review, discuss, and investigate course content with the instructor in class. In this model, lecture content is removed from the classroom to allow time for active learning, and the content that was removed is delivered to students via on-line video. This approach 'flips' the traditional use of lecture and more active learning approaches. Lecture occurs outside of class, and more active learning, such as problem solving, happens during class. Assessment data was collected to examine students' use of the video lectures and perceptions of the classroom flip. The students' feedback suggests that while the active learning and additional project time available in class improved their understanding, they would prefer that only about half the classes be flipped and some use of traditional lectures should be maintained.

Introduction

The flipped classroom describes a reversal of traditional teaching where students gain first exposure to new material outside of class, usually via reading or lecture videos, and then class time is used to do the harder work of assimilating that knowledge through strategies such as problem solving, discussion or debates. The purpose of flipping the classroom is to shift from passive to active learning to focus on the higher order thinking skills such as analysis, synthesis and evaluation.

Roles and Expectations

1. Students take more responsibility for their own learning and study core content either individually or in groups before class and then apply knowledge and skills to a range of activities using higher order thinking
2. Teaching 'one-to-many' focuses more on facilitation and moderation than lecturing, though lecturing is still important. Significant learning opportunities can be gained through facilitating active learning, engaging students, guiding learning, correcting misunderstandings and providing timely feedback using a variety of pedagogical strategies
3. There is a greater focus on concept exploration, meaning making and demonstration or application of knowledge in the face-to-face setting.

Educational Technologies

1. Capture key content for students to access at their own convenience and to suit their pace of learning
2. Present learning materials in a variety of formats to suit different learner styles
3. Provide opportunities for discourse and interaction in and out of class
4. Convey timely information, updates and reminders for students
5. Provide immediate and anonymous feedback for teachers and students to signal revision points
6. Capture data about students to analyze their progress and identify 'at risk' students

Significant of Flipped Classroom

In a traditional lecture, students often try to capture what is being said at the instant the speaker says it. They cannot stop to reflect upon what is being said, and they may miss significant points because they are trying to transcribe the instructor's words. By contrast, the use of video and other prerecorded media puts lectures under the control of the students. They can watch, rewind and fast-forward as needed. This ability may be of particular value to students with accessibility concerns especially where captions are provided for those with hearing impairments. Lectures that can be viewed more than once may also help those for whom English is not their first language. Devoting class time to application of concepts might give instructors a better opportunity to detect errors in thinking, particularly those that are widespread in a class. At the same time, collaborative projects can encourage social interaction among students, making it easier for them to learn from one another and for those of varying skill levels to support their peers. The Flipped Classroom model does not have a true script, however the Flipped Learning network organizations has defined four main pillars associated to the acronym FLIP (Flexible Environment, Learning Culture, Intentional Content, and Professional Educator).

Flexible Environment: Teachers often need to reorganize physically the learning space in order to make it easier for group work, independent study, search, and student evaluation. They may even need to fall back on other physical spaces that are different from the usual classroom: the playground, the canteen, the library or even outide school places (museums, botanic gardens, etc.). Teachers also need to accept that the classroom might be noisier and have more student movement opposed to simple lecturing classes. On the other hand, the flexibility of the classroom should include learning times and evaluation methods. Therefore, teachers are expected to build suitable evaluation methods, establishing objective criteria that are clear, and can be well understood by both the teachers and the students.

Learning Culture: In the traditional model the teacher is the main source of information, the possessor of the wisdom and responsible for "knowledge transfer" to students often using a directive model. In the inverted classroom model, the teacher consciously frees him/herself to the student. The classroom is taken to explore themes in a deeper way, giving rise to richer learning opportunities, more diverse and adjusted to the students' difficulties and needs. The students are actively involved in processing the information, shaping the knowledge through participation opportunities and self evaluation in a significant way. Students can take part or develop pair or larger groups learning activities, like for instance, taking part in learning activities out of the classroom.

Intentional Content: The teacher has to evaluate carefully which content he/she needs to explore in direct teaching and which contents he/she needs to hand out or suggest to students for the self or group study. The teacher needs to know or identify the main competences and difficulties of the students in the subject the contents belong to. His/her also needs to know and identify the access and use conditions of resources and digital technologies by all the students. The goal is to undertake active strategies, draw activities based on problems, done in pairs, for example, and clearly associated with the content to be learnt. It is not meaningless the deep knowledge of what students is able to understand and how they can integrate new concepts with preexisting knowledge.

Professional Educator: In order to use successfully the inverted classroom model, teachers have to be highly professional and qualified, as this model is likely more demanding than the traditional. It is imperative that the teacher understands the optimal moment to use directive teaching or self learning resources. This way the teacher has more time in the classroom to take an individual teaching process and amplifies face-to-face interactions (1:1) between teacher and student and interactions among students. On the other hand, the teacher has to be able to anticipate difficulties the students might face, encouraging questions, motivating and generating learning dynamics both in group or individual and produce or select carefully quality resources that lead to the students' self learning. Also, the teacher has to follow up constantly their students and offer them any immediate and relevant feedback, evaluating continuously their work. The "Flipped" teacher is a reflexive professional in his/her practices, a teacher who can manage his/her lesson plan in a flexible way, and is able to deal with any unforeseeable dynamics in the classroom, taking into account different learning rhythms, contributions, interests and problems the students might arise with. Before adopting the Flipped Classroom model the teacher has to make sure that the students with whom he/she is going to work have the necessary access conditions and adequate knowledge in what technologies are concerned and the necessary digital services to develop the activities. The teacher also needs to check if there are any special needs students in such a way that he/she can promote adequate access conditions and digital access of the educational resources as well as the need of supportive devices to the use of technology (hardware and software).

The Implications for Teaching and Learning

The flipped classroom constitutes a role change for instructors, who give up their front-of-the-class position in favor of a more collaborative and cooperative contribution to the teaching process. There is a concomitant change in the role of students, many of whom are used to being cast as passive participants in the education process, where instruction is served to them. The flipped model puts more of the responsibility for learning on the shoulders of students while giving them greater impetus to experiment. Activities can be student led and communication among students can become the determining dynamic of a session devoted to learning through hands on work. What the flip does particularly well is to bring about a distinctive shift in priorities from merely covering material to working toward mastery of flipped class.

Conclusion

This new model is challenging teachers to reflect on their practice and rethink how they reach their students. It is an approach that encourages students to set the pace for truly individualized instruction. It is a catalyst for teachers, administrators, and students to change the way things have always been done.

32

Flipped Learning - Teaching for Tomorrow

Flipped classrooms are shifting the way of traditional teaching methods to engage students in the learning process. Using technology, lectures are moved out of the classroom and delivered online as a means to free up class time for interaction and collaboration. In order to effectively implement a flipped classroom, teachers must possess a set of requisite technical skills, conceptual knowledge and pedagogical expertise. Through this study, web-based information was collected to prospective teachers interested in implementing a flipped classroom. This paper throws light on an overview of the required material, working implementations to raise the confidence level of the participants. It would support the learning community, either in-person or online, would help to provide guidance through initiation and expand on the shared experiences of the individuals.

Introduction

As technologies and broadband become more widely available and as the focus on integrating technology into learning increases, interest in Flipped Learning will likely continue to grow. In the Flipped Learning model, teachers shift direct learning out of the large group learning space and move it into the individual learning space, with the help of one of several technologies. Teachers record and narrate screen casts of work they do on their computer desktops, create videos of themselves teaching, or curate video lessons from internet sites.

Salient Features of Flipped Learning

Teachers also can use class time to check on each student's understanding and, if necessary, help them develop procedural fluency.

Teachers can provide individualized support as students work through the activities designed to help them master the material, meeting them at their readiness level.

How Does it Differ from Other Learning?

1. Flipped Learning has been compared to online, blended, and distance learning because of the screen cast or video components, but, there are clear differences.
2. Online education occurs only remotely, and the teacher and student are never face-to-face.
3. Virtual class meetings, assignments, and lectures happen online through a course management website usually, but not always, asynchronously.
4. Sometimes the lectures and other activities are augmented by group chats or other means of facilitating collaboration and peer instruction.
5. Blended classes also have an online element, but that usually occurs during class time along with direct student-teacher contact.
6. Flipped Learning model can enable educators to make the shift from teacher-driven instruction to student-centered learning.

Four Pillars of Flipped Learning

1. Flexible Environment,
2. Learning Culture,
3. Intentional Content, and
4. Professional Educator.
   (a) Flipped Learning Requires Flexible Environments
   (b) Flipped Learning Requires A Shift In Learning Culture
   (c) Flipped Learning Requires Intentional Content
   (d) Flipped Learning Requires Professional Educators

Active Learning

Teacher-centered models focus on the acquisition of knowledge outside of the context and instructional delivery includes lecture, homework, and exams, used for assigning grades. Little time is allotted for teachers to work directly with students to guide them as they attempt to meaningfully apply the information. This approach has been described as a "one-size-fits-all" model of instruction, in which effective teaching is characterized as presenting information well, and those who can learn, will learn. In contrast, teachers using a student-centered approach engage students in actively constructing knowledge and they work together to evaluate students' learning

Diverse Learners

In the flipped classroom, the teacher moves lower levels of the taxonomy to outside of the group learning space, where students can then work on mastering concepts on their own time and pace. When using video, students can pause, rewind, and review the lesson at any time. In class, the teacher and students can then focus on the upper levels of the taxonomy (applying, analyzing, and creating.)

This has potentials to allow struggling learners more opportunities to understand and improve their recall before they come to class, as previously described in the research on cognitive load.

Concerns about Flipped Learning

1. Some have argued that Flipped Learning is not a defined model and the result of teachers using different tools to meet individual students' needs. This is a valid observation. The flipped classroom model does not eliminate the lecture or other means of direct instruction.
2. It removes lectures from the group learning space to maximize the amount of time teachers have to spend with individual students and students have to spend working with one another.
3. Flipping the classroom provides more time to address the needs of individual students and enables more active and engaged learning, without sacrificing the amount of material that can be covered.
4. It is true that the Flipped Learning model is not the only way to facilitate good teaching.
5. It is important to note that Flipped Learning might not work for all educators and students or with all grades and subject matters. Not all educators will succeed with it and some students may prefer traditional classroom approaches.

Conclusion

Flipped classrooms have the opportunity to cause a significant shift in the way instruction is delivered. Using technology, teachers are now able to provide an alternative to traditional lecture-based models by implementing a blended learning method that combines the benefits of direct instruction and active learning to engage students in the learning process.

The method requires a set of technical skills, conceptual knowledge and pedagogical expertise to implement effectively. Delivering those skills through a single module is best accomplished through a broad approach that provides users with an overview of the method and gives them the proper skills and expertise to get started.

To enhance their knowledge, participants must be exposed to working examples within their area of instruction to build confidence in their ability to implement the method on their own. Access to support communities should also be made available to provide guidance and expand on the learned experiences shared by their peers.

Lectures are a time-honored method for engaging students, conveying information, and posing questions. The lecture format sometimes includes opportunities for students to ask or answer questions. Yet data-driven research on teaching and learning has long indicated that the lecture is only one way to engage students in learning. Other teaching approaches promote and advance student learning while responding effectively to changes in student and faculty demographics. Teaching scholars have successfully explored non-tech, low-tech, and high-tech ways to apply these research findings in their courses.

References

1. www.uw.edu/teaching
2. "The Flipped Classroom FAQ" Center for the Integration of Research, Teaching and Learning. Sept 2012. http://www.cirtl.net/node/7788
3. Implementing a Flipped Classroom: An Instructional Module- Dean N. Shimamoto
4. www.flippedlearning.org.

33

Usage of Internet for Education Purpose Among Arts and Science College

Introduction

Education plays an important role in building a creative society. Due to the revolutionary changes in the field of telecommunications and Information Technology, educational institutions may be transformed from "teaching centers" to "centers of learning resources". Language is a tool for communication, and the system of language is learned for the purpose of communication (Clark, 1978).Internet is also a tool for effective communication among the several developments in Information and Communication Technology. The usage of Internet, social network, you tube; etc will stimulate the creativity among the users. Usage of internet for hi-tech innovative learning will develop the creativity of the students.

Need and Significance of the Study

Developing a creative society is the worldwide objective in education. Internet learning allows the learners to have more control over their own learning to think creatively, analytically, critically and to work collaboratively. The role of internet communication mediums have increased in social and academic interpersonal communications(Huang,2010).However, the internet usage among the students for learning is considerably less due to lack of Internet facilities and skills. The purpose of using Internet has an impact upon the innovative learning of the students.

Student teachers are enrolled only from Arts and Science colleges. As a Teacher educator, to promote the hi-tech knowledge of student teachers, we should evaluate and know about the technology skill of students from Arts and Science colleges, so that we can plan hi-tech oriented curriculum for our student teachers. Hence the investigator feels the need to study the usage of Internet by students' population from Arts and Science colleges. The 'usage' is referred to as practical use of Internet application in day to day educational activities by Arts and Science College students. Five major Internet communication modes (i.e.websites, e-mail, social network, YouTube and blogs) were considered in this study.

Objectives

1. To find out the level of Internet usage by the students of Arts and Science colleges.
2. To find out whether there is significant differences in the usage of Internet by the students of Arts and Science colleges in terms of the variables namely

    (a) Gender

    (b) Subject of study group

    (c) Location of college

    (d) Nature of the college

    (e) Annual income of Parents.

Hypotheses

1. The level of Internet usage among the students of Arts and Science colleges is high.
2. There is significant difference in the usage of Internet among the students of Arts and Science colleges in terms of

    1. Gender

2. Subject of study group
3. Location of the college
4. Nature of the college
5. Annual income of Parents.

Sample

A sample of 160 Arts and Science college students belonging to five colleges in Madurai in Tamil Nadu was selected for the study. Samples were selected by **proportionate stratified representative** sample techniques. To achieve the objectives of the study **survey method** of the research was used.

Tool Used

The tool consisted of 30 statements under 5 dimensions anchored with 5-point rating scale [often, as and when needed some time, Rarely, Never] to indicate the level of acceptance of students. The minimum and maximum scores of the scale were 30 and 150 respectively. The tool was finalized with consultation of the teacher educators and research experts. Reliability and validity of the tool was established.

Data Collection Procedure

The purpose of the study was explained to the students and ample time was given to go through the tool and doubts were clarified while administrating the tool.

Statistical Techniques

Mean, Standard Deviation, and t-test.

Results

(i) Mean

No of Samples	Theoretical Mean	Calculated Mean
160	90	92.59

(ii) Mean Value under Dimension

S.No	Dimensions	Mean
1	Websites	23.41
2	e-mail	21.26
3	Social network	19.48
4	You tube	19.43
5	Blogs	9

(iii) Level of Significance:

S.No	Variables	Category	N	Mean	S D	't' Value	0.05 level of Significance
1	Gender	Male Female	80 80	92.96 89.13	11.92 11.63	2.054	**Significant.**
2	Subject of study group	Computer science Other subjects	80 80	91.45 88.23	10.62 10.02	1.973	**Significant.**
3	Nature of the college	Aided Self Finance	80 80	93.213 90.362	10.93 11.02	1.720	**Not Significant**
4	Location of the college	Urban Rural	80 80	91.62 88.11	11.73 11.52	1.909	**Not Significant**
5	Annual income of Parents	Above 3 lakhs Below 3 lakhs	75 85	93.97 11.65	90.14 12.81	1.984	**Significant**

Findings

1. The mean value of Internet usage among the students of Arts and Science College is **high.**
2. The results obtained from mean value of different dimensions show that the majority usage of internet is through **Websites** and least usage is through **Blogs.**
3. There is **significant difference** between **male and female** students of Arts and Science colleges in the usage of Internet for educational purposes. The result is in favour of **male group.**
4. There is **significant difference** between **computer science and other subject group** students of Arts and Science colleges

in the usage of Internet for educational purpose. The result is in favour of computer science group students.

5. There is **no significant difference** between the students of **Aided and Self finance** Arts and Science colleges in the usage of Internet for educational purpose.
6. There is no **significant difference** between students of **Rural and Urban** Arts and Science colleges in the usage of Internet for educational purpose.
7. There is **significant difference** in the usage of Internet for educational purpose between the students of Arts and Science colleges whose parents' annual income is below and above Rs.3Lacks.The result is in favour of students whose Parents' annual income is **above 3 lakhs**.

Suggestions for Educational Implication

From this research findings here are some suggestions for improving the usage of Internet.

1. As Internet has become an integral part in today's education, well-equipped infrastructure such as computer lab with Internet facility is essential in every institution.
2. The Internet usage payment in colleges should be providing at concession rate for the students.
3. The syllabi should have some online based learning topics for students.
4. All teachers should communicate with their students by using Internet mode.
5. All major students other than computer science should learn ICT oriented courses in a compulsory manner.
6. Parents should give opportunity to their children, [particularly female] for using Internet for their studies.
7. To encourage on line communication, teacher should encourage the students to submit their assignments only through e-mail, blogs, etc.

8. The university should organize the technology oriented enrichment programmes for all students and teachers.

Conclusion

Only hi-tech knowledge can promote the creative society nowadays. Tremendous changes in education can occur through advanced technologies used inside the classroom. Only the teacher can develop the digital knowledge among students in all levels. Therefore the investigator suggests that apart from class room teaching, teachers should involve themselves in creative techno instruction and encourage the students to develop their software knowledge.

References

1. Jyotsna saxena, Manoj kumar saxena, Sandhya Gihar, ICT in Professional Education, A.P.H. Publishing corporation, 2010, New DELHI.
2. Kamatchi, ICT For Social Change, Edutracks, Vol.11-No.12, Aug, 2012
3. Parthasarathy, Ananthasayanum, Ravi, Usage of Internet Applications among B.Ed students, Edutracks, Vol.12-No.7, March, 2013.